LIFE WITH BONDO, OUR COTTAGE ON WHEELS

Lynn & Doreen Lyndore

MINERVA PRESS

LONDON
MONTREUX   LOS ANGELES   SYDNEY

First Published 1998 by
MINERVA PRESS
195, Knightsbridge
London SW7 1RE

Printed and bound in Great Britain by
Antony Rowe Ltd, Chippenham, Wiltshire

LIFE WITH BONDO, OUR COTTAGE ON WHEELS

The park at Bath

We dedicate this book to
Denise and Alexandre

Met by chance
On the top of a pass,
Unbeknown then
From what followed hence
This book could be penned.

Foreword

This book is not a guide book, nor is it a diary, as it does not follow a sequence of events – it is rather the story of a way of life and a hotchpotch of experiences. We offer no excuse for any confusion that may arise either geographically or time-wise, because our life and travels with Bondo have already spanned more than twenty summers and almost as many countries in Western Europe.

Was it by coincidence – or shall we call it destiny? – that on our retirement after a lifetime of hard work, financial limitations and routine that our chance meeting with Bondo led to her becoming our 'home on wheels', from where the world passes by our windows.

This way of life affords us a sense of complete freedom and utter irresponsibility. Nobody knows where we are and nobody cares. Mail does not reach us because we can give no forwarding address as our forward movements are mostly unknown and unplanned, even what country we will be in has no precise date. Every day is a voyage of discovery, whether we travel the miles or the yards or remain static. There are new experiences every day, new vistas, changing environment and ever changing weather, and last, but certainly not least, personal encounters and new friends.

A way of travel – sans suitcases, sans schedules, sans bookings, sans trains and planes; no ever-changing hotel beds, even when we visit friends we sleep in our own beds; no need for restaurants, we eat and entertain 'at home'; and none of those expenses, only the cost of the food we prepare 'at home' and the petrol we need to move from here to there. Even the cost of a repair, not infrequent, costs far less than a few days in an hotel.

Our way of travel is not only going from here to there, it is rather a living here and a living there.

Our home is where we take it, wherever we choose to be or where chance leads – on the mountains and in the valleys; by rivers, canals, lakes, lochs, loughs, fjords and the seas; on hills and plains or in forests; farms, villages, towns and cities, as well as the capitals of Europe – country lanes, secondary roads, highways, and when absolutely unavoidable, motorways, from which we escape as fast as we can. The busy streets of cities in which we lose our way and our sense of direction, especially when we try the narrow side streets and find ourselves diverted by *senso unico* (one way) – how often we have experienced kindness from considerate motorists and cyclists who have gone out of their way to put us in the right direction by saying "follow me!"

Inevitably there is the hunt to find somewhere to park either for sightseeing or to have a meal – and at the end of the day somewhere to rest our wheels for the night, with a view from the windows for my early morning sketches.

Yes, Bondo, as you see from her portrait, is a motor-caravan – or Dormobile as defined by her trade name. How we came to name her Bondo, the first Swiss village we came to after crossing the Italian border into the Bregalia Valley, we tell in another chapter.

For us two sisters Bondo is a way of life.

Ullswater

Contents

Prologue

Bondo Our Cottage

Home is our cottage wherever we roam
In our cottage on wheels we are always at home.
Home is our cottage on the shores of the seas,
By rivers and lakes and beneath the trees.
On the sides of fjords, by quiet lochs,
On harbour piers and ferry quays.

Home is our cottage on the sands of the beach
Where we sport in the waves within easy reach,
Or drop into the lake in the heat of the day
Before driving on to continue our way.

At home in our cottage on the Venetian lagoon
At dawn, at sunset, and at the full moon.
Far in the North we are also at home
On the archipelago of Stockholm.
In wonderful, wonderful Copenhagen
The little mermaid is in our front garden.

20/7/74

PALAZZA DORMOBILI.
LIDO VENICE.

"Palazzo Dormobili" at the Lido in Venice.

Stockholm

Home is our cottage on the polderdam,
On the city canals of Amsterdam,
On little canals, on the farms of France,
On the banks of Europe's waterways
We watch the barges gliding past.

In capital cities with churches and towers,
Their beautiful parks, fine trees and bright flowers,
In Luxembourg, London, Paris and Bern
We stay on and on to sightsee and learn.
At home when we park in a city street
And often stay on for more than a week;
And in city parks from Bergen to Bath
We can comfortably park on a tree-lined path.

Home in our cottage on cathedral squares,
Zaragoza, Ravenna, Bourges, Rheims and Wells
At dawn we awake to the chimes of the bells.
In the countryside when time to search
For somewhere to sleep there's the village church.
In our friends' driveway
No trouble at all,
We are welcome to stay.

On the pier on Lac Leman on the French–Swiss border.

Youghal fishing harbour, Eire.

At the castle gate at Powys in Wales,
In the grounds of châteaux and stately homes,
On lonely moors and haunted vales
Up the hills and down the dales,
On the top of a pass
Near the mountain peak
We are always at home.

In swirling mists, 'neath soft snow flakes,
With driving rain and pelting hail.
Even in Athens that time
In the burning heat of the Grecian clime
We were also at home.

A problem we have when it's nearly dark,
There is nowhere in sight where we can park.
We find ourselves on a great highway
With polluting monsters roaring by,
This is a time of deep despair
When travel becomes a bad nightmare.
A time to make a hasty retreat
To creep inside a field of wheat
Or hide ourselves in a forest deep
Where nightingales sing us to sleep.

Home is our cottage wherever we roam
In our cottage on wheels we are always at home.

A New Way of Life

From the very beginning of our experience with Bondo we have again and again had reason to ponder on those age-old questions – fate, destiny or merely coincidence? This is the theme which is almost part of our lives with Bondo.

We often wonder why I made that sudden detour to pay a surprise visit to my cousin who was working at an artist's gallery in the ancient harbour area at Caesarea. Was it sheer chance that her friend called in while I was there and quite casually mentioned that her cousin from New Zealand, who had been travelling in Europe in a motor-caravan, was staying in a kibbutz not far from our home town? As a mere afterthought she suggested that I might make his acquaintance.

A few days later I went out to the kibbutz – there she was, parked in the shade of enormous eucalyptus trees. It was a case of love at first sight! I was welcomed in – it was indeed a whole cottage on wheels with even an oak-panelled dining room. I was intrigued!

When, some weeks later, I was invited to be his guide on a tour of Israel my enthusiasm knew no bounds. There followed lovely days and nights on the shores of the Sea of Galilee, up on to the Golan Heights, down through the deep rift of the Jordan Valley to Jericho; up to Jerusalem, parked at night on Mount Zion with a view of the City – old and new.

We continued down the Rift Valley along the Dead Sea, and down the Sinai coast to its most southerly point at Ras Mahamoud. I remember how we cooked in our kitchen the snow-white fish that divers had given us. With all the comforts of home we were able to live on the beaches, the days spent snorkelling among the coral reefs, swimming among the multi-coloured tropical fish. Even in mid-summer we were able to live in the desert – the secret was to face the caravan in the direction that would catch the sea breezes.

On our return from the desert we made for Caesarea – we had tickets for the visiting British Royal Ballet performing at the Roman amphitheatre. We just had time to dine and dress. After the performance the rest of the audience departed for their homes. We remained parked on the cliff and slept to the sound of the waves breaking against the rocks and the ruins of the ancient harbour.

I had really learnt that home is where you take it and that you are at home just wherever you want to be. I then knew that I wanted to possess this caravan more than anything else on earth.

It was a couple of months later that for business reasons the Kiwi had to return urgently to New Zealand and asked us to take the caravan back to England for him. We could not leave before the end of the academic year, so poor Bondo spent six miserable months in bond in a dirty garage approved of by Customs (it had been difficult to find storage that would take her height, a problem often to be encountered in the future).

Sometime after his return to New Zealand Kiwi wrote that he wanted to settle down and "go no more a-roaming". At his request we transferred the purchase price to the Soldiers' Welfare Fund – and Bondo was ours!

And so, one memorable day in June, Bondo and ourselves were released from bondage – for ourselves it was the beginning of our retirement, for Bondo her release from the six miserable months in bondage where she was committed by order of the Customs. At last she stood before our door and the great preparations began for our long awaited departure.

A few days later we drove down to the harbour and Bondo was swung aboard and fastened down on the deck (the car-hold headroom was too low on that ship). So we started life 'at home' in our luxury 'stateroom' with all 'port holes' looking out to sea. Needless to say we had no need of the seat accommodation we had been obliged to pay for on the good ship *Appolonia*. How we missed our luxury cabin on future trips to join Bondo, back and forth on ship accommodation that deteriorated from year to year – for we could only afford seat passages.

We did not go ashore at Cyprus the next day, but the following day went ashore at Rhodes as it was necessary to victual Bondo. We had been so busy cleaning and packing our household that there had been no time for shopping. We found excellent food shops and a number of familiar British products within the walls of the old town – and to the surprise of the shopkeepers (they knew we were from the ship) proceeded to purchase not only current requirements but also basic stores. Overladen, we returned on board and organised our kitchen cupboards.

The next day we relaxed 'at home' and at night we were rocked to sleep on our own springs and the gentle swells of a Mediterranean summer sea.

On arrival at Piraeus Bondo was swung out from the deck – there were some moments of agony as she dangled in mid-air, one of us watching from the deck above and the other from the dock below – a sigh of relief as she landed with a gentle bump on her wheels. Out of the harbour we drove with no more formality than – did we have firearms?

"Should we?"

We followed the road sign for Athens, and so began our lives in Europe, appropriately at the very cradle of Western civilisation.

After all these years the memory of that arrival is still exciting. It was for us the beginning of a new way of life.

Bondo's dining room

Heading North

We had spent our first days in Athens, battling the midsummer heat, living in the pine woods below the Acropolis – spending many hours at the Parthenon and among the ruins of the Agora, and also at the museums, obtaining a more detailed picture than time previously spent on brief visits to Athens.

Reluctant as we were to leave Greece, living in Bondo in midsummer was a bad start for our 'new way of life', so we decided to head north to more temperate climes.

We spent two days skirting the Corinth coast, cooling down in the refreshing waters of the Isthmus, until we reached Patras from where we sailed to Ancona on the Italian coast. There we lazed for many days close to the sea living on the velvet sands of the Adriatic.

After enjoying the wonders of Ravenna we headed north along the coast through Choggia, that Little Venice, and along Nuovo Strada Romea, the causeway across the islands which so well illustrates how Venice was built.

Arriving in Venice in time for the Festa del Redentore, the regatta on the Giudecca Canal and concerts on St Mark's Square with memories of previous visits to this most unique of all cities in the world; the first time in the days of our youth together, and now together again with Bondo.

On arrival we immediately made for the ferryboat to take us and Bondo across the lagoon to the Lido Di Venezia where we intended to take up residence. How excited we were as we sailed through St Mark's Basin with our cottage. Incidentally, NO CAMPING ALLOWED ON THE LIDO – but we do not camp. We find a plot for our cottage, the price of which we do not have to consider: our stipulation is only that it must have a view.

For the first two nights we stayed in a tree-lined avenue, the Avenue Lamberti, but then decided that it was rather dark because the enormous plane trees met overhead and there was no really good view. So after some reconnoitring we found the perfect plot, as neighbours of palazzo dwellers, on the edge of the lagoon gazing west across to Venice – one of the most attractive skylines imaginable, from where in the early dawn we watched the city rising from the mists and in the evenings experienced the glorious sunsets when we came home early enough. From the Lido each day we took a vaporetto to Venice where we saw all the usual sights as well as spending many hours on St Mark's Square. There is always something going on in Venice and mostly one can enjoy the happenings for free as many take place on the Square. It costs money to sit down on the Square except, of course, around the flagstaffs in front of the Basilica and the two columns near the waterfront next to the Doge's Palace. On this occasion we arrived early to take our places on the steps of one of the columns for a ringside seat for the fireworks which were to open the Festa. The crowds, as always, were immense – the early evening promenaders filling the square – and on this occasion, as for most special occasions, the four enormous flags were flying in front of the Basilica (I remembered so well witnessing the arrival of Queen Elizabeth and the Duke of Edinburgh, who came ashore here from the Royal Yacht Britannia anchored in the Basin; and how the crowds surged through the police cordons – and the evening firework display – an indescribable scene across the water, finalised by lights in bottles floating across from Giudecca). We have seen the flags at full spread in the breeze or just hanging limply.

It is just as well to look up to the flags as quite often the Square is littered with papers and lounging hippies – but it is always exciting. One invariably makes for St Mark's Square on arrival in Venice and stays on and on until the night turns cold and one catches cold too, usually being insufficiently clad.

After the gorgeous display of fireworks, for which Venice is so eminently suitable, we were treated to a most delightful orchestral concert, after which a brass band took over. After the musicians had departed, the light classical café orchestras drew the standing populace while their tables had only a sprinkling of customers – but thanks to these orchestras the sound of music floats across the Square for many hours of the day and night.

A new and rather surprising sight in St Mark's Square at midday is to see tourists in the outdoor cafés of the famous Florian and the other restaurants ordering a beer or tea or coffee and opening their lunch packets; this, of course, is because the cost of restaurant meals has skyrocketed so. Who would have dared, a few years ago, to eat one's fish and chips or chicken bones at those illustrious tables on St Mark's Square, 'The Salon of Europe', to the strains of classical music?

We, of course, do not dare to order even a drink or beverage there – it would cost us a whole day's food budget!

Next day the Gondola Race was scheduled. Doreen was certain that it would take place along the Grand Canal – I thought along the Giudecca, so as a compromise we decided to take a pew at the Salute, which protrudes into both canals. We went fairly early, again to secure a ringside view, and found only a dozen or so people about and could not understand why. Finally, someone confirmed that the Giudecca Canal would be the course and that the gondolas would not be coming round into the Grand Canal. We should have known better as the Festa was named for the Redentore, the church on the Giudecca island. So back we went on No. 1 vaporetto, which plies the Grand Canal, to the landing stage at Zaccaria to take No. 5 across to Giudecca. As one was at the pier when we arrived there I jumped on as it was drawing away and to my horror found that Doreen had been left behind without a single lira in her purse (I had the tickets and all the money). To add to my stupidity the vaporetto went in the wrong direction, so I disembarked at the next station and awaited a return vaporetto and found her still waiting at the Zaccaria pier. It was then decided that we would both carry money with us. The incident gave us a good laugh anyway. Another less amusing vaporetto incident was when my spectacles fell into the canal. I had a habit of wearing my specs on my head, and as I leaned back for some reason or other the glasses flew off my head into the water. The dirty canals, which most visitors to Venice say smell, did not invite jumping off the vaporetto to rescue them!

By the time we reached the Giudecca the race was almost over. We saw only the finish, but what a colourful sight – the gondoliers in their straw hats and striped jerseys and sleek black gondolas followed by their supporters in all sorts of craft. However, the most exciting part was the festive atmosphere and the noisy banter of the gondoliers and their fans.

During our fortnight's stay on the Lido di Venezia we attended for the first time the weekly markets set up in town squares and streets and which we were to encounter many times on our travels. The Lido market was particularly interesting as the vendors have to come across the lagoon either with their pantechnicons and lorries on the ferryboat or bring their goods by barge. In the pre-dawn we awoke to see barges drawing up on the shore a few yards from Bondo and offloading their goods. We knew about smugglers coming ashore at lonely coves and, not knowing about the market, were puzzled at the activity. These street markets open at 7 a.m. and pack up at noon and arrive at their next town or village early next morning. In Venice, there is of course the permanent Rialto market known to all visitors; the vendors there also pack up at the end of the day.

While waiting in the queue to board the ferryboat on our departure from the Lido and Venice, a young Swiss couple, the girl very beautiful, waiting in a car behind us, started speaking to us in English as they noted our British number plates. We do not mind how long we wait on ferry piers as we are 'at home', so as the queue in front was still very long we invited them in for coffee. We were grateful for their warning us against travelling over the Brenner Pass into Austria because the traffic and accident rate is horrendous. They invited us to contact them should we come to Zurich, as they would like to show us around their city.

How we enjoyed that last look at Venice as we glided through St Mark's Basin and up the Giudecca Canal which had become so much part of ourselves in the past fortnight.

Coming back and forth to Bondo over the years we have stayed over in Venice many times – never quite the same as being 'at home' in Venice in Bondo.

Northward Bound from Venice

Our next objective was open-air opera in the Roman amphitheatre in Verona. We arrived in Verona at about 4 p.m. after an unpleasantly hot drive along the main road to Milan, to find that only black-market tickets were available for that evening's performance of *Carmen*. As the afternoon wore on the heat wave became more and more intense – we spent our time drinking *grifiti* (crushed ice and peppermint) – the most wonderful drink which we have never seen again, certainly not sold at kiosks as it is in Verona. Our Bondo is not habitable under conditions of extreme heat, and we have no frigidaire to provide us even with cold drinks.

So we decided to set off towards Lake Garda. We did not know what main road we were on, but that Saturday evening the traffic was even worse than that which we had struck in Athens on the Sunday of our arrival. We finally reached Laseze, at the south end of the Lake, and found it so overcrowded that we drove into the nearest car park and decided that we had had enough for that day.

The noise of traffic on the main road adjoining the car park kept us awake most of the night and we became so depressed that we asked ourselves – "Is our journey really necessary?" We wondered what we were letting ourselves in for. We have had moments since then – always reaction to heavy traffic and heat and noise – but we have never again reached such a low ebb. Next morning, at 4 a.m., well before dawn, we drove on to Brescia where we parked in a shady avenue near the castle and slept nearly all day. Later in the afternoon we took a stroll in the old town and saw some of its historic buildings – and then we saw *it* – a bill-board advertising a ballet performance that evening on the lake at Sirmione, some twenty miles back to Lake Garda from Brescia.

We went into the nearest café and asked them to phone for us, to reserve seats for the performance, hoping that there were still some available. There were! We duly found ourselves in the attractive resort of Sirmione, a peninsula jutting into La Garda with a moat drawbridge leading to the old walled town. We were intrigued. Armed with the tickets purchased at the tourist office we crossed the moat by the drawbridge and made our way to the 'theatre', at least one thousand yards away, where the stage was built out into the water and the 'auditorium' was on the rocks at the water's edge. We grabbed folding wooden chairs and looked for a good vantage point – preferably on a raised bit of rock.

The stage was draped with a fishing net as backdrop and the dancer, Carla Fracci, the prima ballerina from La Scala, suddenly appeared on the stage with the backdrop lit up and we enjoyed a breathtaking, dreamlike performance for the entire evening by this wonderful ballerina – perfect renderings of dances from Pandora's Box, Swan Lake, etc. and finally the most beautiful interpretation of the Dying Swan we have ever seen – her arm movements were perfection.

After each dance the lighting effects on the net gave us glimpses of her changing costumes and putting on her ballet shoes. At the interval she crossed to the mainland along a long narrow footbridge especially built – everything blacked out with the spotlight on the dancer as she floated along the bridge waving to the ecstatic audience. During the dancing, spotlights played on yachts with coloured sails gliding behind the stage. This performance, balletomanes that we are, remains in our memories as among the most thrilling events in our travels.

Only twenty-four hours earlier, in a state of deepest depression, we had asked ourselves whether our journey was really necessary. Was it?

We returned to Bondo, parked in the tree-lined avenue of Sirmione, and it was now necessary to find a suitable place to spend the night. After driving around for a while we finally came to the parking area adjoining the modern Congress Hall, surrounded by lawns and trees and shrubs. At dawn we were awakened by a shower of rain, and Lynn found water leaking on to her bed – this was the first intimation of the damage to the roof of Bondo sustained on the Hill of the Muses hunting for a tree to give a little shade from the intense heat. But the 'rain' turned out to be the garden sprays which the gardeners had turned on. We turned Bondo around for the sprays to give her a bath on the other side as well. She was filthy and needed the wash.

After bathing ourselves in our big basin and partaking of breakfast, we left this enchanting place and went to Desenzano to look for the Automobile Association for some advice on the best route to take to Switzerland. There was no parking to be found, so we double-parked outside the Touring Club offices when an English woman, seeing our GB registration came up to us. A most charming person, married to an Italian, they live in Milan and have a summer cottage in Sirmione and so are well versed on the area. She recommended that we make for Lake Iseo and take the route up the west side, as the east side is too mountainous. We were grateful to this woman for her advice as we found Lake Iseo idyllic.

After a pleasant drive we reached the southern end of Lake Iseo at about 2 p.m. and we had lunch and a swim. As we drove northwards a gorgeous scene opened up – a high island, in fact a mountain peak rising up in the middle of the lake and all around high mountains; and then we arrived at the village of Riva. We parked Bondo and had a look at this one-street village on the water's edge. Behind the road the church and a few houses climbed upwards. Two attractive blondes from the pub were serving customers in the open-air, creeper-covered café across the road. We decided that this was where we would stay the night and go into the pub during the evening to watch the life of the locals. But first we must find our suitable 'view' before the evening closes in. We drove out of the village and within a couple of hundred yards we found the perfect 'camp' – a green sward under big trees at the lake edge with the lovely view across it. For a while we watched the fishermen laying their nets from their boats, afterwards we walked back to the village.

We came upon a shop selling all manner of camping equipment and examined a torch lamp because we badly needed suitable lighting for reading at night. We did not dare use the caravan lights for fear of running down the battery as we did not relish the idea of having to push our cottage to get the engine started. In fact it would be quite impossible for us to move that heavy vehicle. The lamp cost 4,300 lire – an expense we could not bear without sleeping over the decision. So off we went to the pub.

We had no sooner walked in when the blondes introduced us to two of the village drunks with a view to matchmaking and a good laugh at our expense. The men were made to buy us drinks and the blondes sat us all down at a table and started up the music. One man, aged about fifty and as tight as an owl, attached himself to Do and invited her to dance. The other, about seventy or more, toothless and decrepit, and so drunk that he could hardly stand, did not show any interest in me – he was much too interested in one of the blonde barmaids. She said he was her uncle. The two girls were enjoying the joke immensely because Do's cavalier was becoming most amorous. The Campari drink they gave us was most potent and such a terrible taste that I could not stomach it. We had not been asked what we wanted to drink – they were thrust upon us. I suppose it was the cheapest dope in the pub. Do, by this time, was getting rather tipsy on her empty stomach – we had not eaten since lunch-time – and for this reason she was, no doubt, able to put up with the admirer. After all, she had made a conquest, it was amusing, and there was no common language.

When we had had enough we somehow managed to extricate ourselves, but were careful to cover our tracks as we did not want the men to see where we were spending the night. We had no desire to have the Don Juans prowling around. We had already had one rather unpleasant experience at Mascerata with youths trying to peep in and a grown man standing around for a long time, whom we had concluded was a sex maniac because of his actions.

Having given our Iseo friends the slip we decided to enjoy this spot for a couple of days. Again in the early morning we observed the dawn across the lake and the fishermen going out to draw in their nets with the night's catch. We were to enjoy many hours all over Europe watching the life of fishermen – those quiet and relaxed scenes which, I suppose, were the reasons for our fascination. We had not yet taken to fishing ourselves, but we did later in Norway – albeit not exactly successfully.

After breakfast we did our laundering in the lake, and even washed our hair. Early in the morning the lake waters were calm and Do went in for a swim, but later they became quite turbulent and as we did not know whether it was safe to bathe at that spot we refrained from further swimming.

Later in the day we walked back to the village shop, decided against the lamp and we saw a colourful two-piece bathing costume which Do bought for 4,300 lire, the price for the lamp we could not afford! We did not think we were too old to wear two-piece costumes. I still wore my Swiss one, purchased when two-piece bathing costumes first became the mode in the Fifties.

How Bondo got her Name

At this point we must project a little into the future as we have referred to our caravan by her name 'Bondo' and must explain how she came to be thus christened.

At first, she had many names. We called her 'The Temple' that first night in Greece when we slept in the pinewoods near the Temple of the Muses on the hill below the Acropolis. In Italy she became '*Palazzo Dormobili*', most appropriate when we resided among the aristocrats at the Lido in Venice, but not so among the beach cabins on the Adriatic coast We called her 'The Chalet' in Switzerland, but that was hardly fitting when we lived in Lausanne, Geneva or Bern.

'The Cottage' was right for most parts of Britain, but not for our town house on the parking lots of tube stations in London. 'The Hutte' seemed suitable for Scandinavia when living on the edge of the fjords in Norway, on the sea front in Denmark or the forests and lakes of Sweden, but not so suitable in the capitals of Oslo, Copenhagen or Stockholm. 'The Château' in France, for town or country; even in Paris our address was as pretentious as that. She had even been named 'The Elephant' by neighbours when she was parked under black plastic wraps in the driveway of a suburban house in a small Somerset town.

But these perpetual name changes were in no way suitable and really quite out of character. It is Bondo who is always the same, she never changes. She remains our modest little home on wheels wherever she is. It is the scenery, the country and the location that changes – she had to have her own name. We cannot refer to her as our caravan, or motor-caravan, she is far more personal and we are so humanly involved with her, a dimension in our lives with 'whom' we have come to have a deep affection. So it was not easy to find just the right name.

We had travelled far and wide for several summers when the revelation came to us both, almost simultaneously. *bondo* – that was the right name from every point of view. Bondo is a Swiss village in the Bregalia Valley, just across from the Italian border where we spent our very first night on Swiss soil. The village lies at the base of the Bondasca gap with views up to the Bergell Massif and is the natural border between Italy and Switzerland. The groves of chestnut trees become less frequent and the vines and fruit trees disappear and the Alpine vegetation takes over. We are in Switzerland. The village is so beautiful that its very memory fills us with nostalgia: its heavy log-built houses with roofs of rough grey stone, deep eaves overhanging the narrow winding lanes, and, like a vain woman who wears many jewels, it is bedecked with cascades of brilliant coloured flowers hanging from every balcony and window. Even the fountains gushing into rough-hewn wooden troughs are bedecked with flowers.

From the village of Bondo we walked for the first time in real European forests, met our first red deer, climbed for the first time above the tree-line and gazed on the glistening face of our first glacier. The next day, on the opposite side of the valley we walked for the first time in upper Alpine pastures "with flowers beneath our feet".

After leaving the village of Bondo we drove on to climb our first Alpine pass – the Maloja, two thousand feet and nine hairpin bends in two miles. Though we were sweating in the bitter cold as we reached the top of the pass Bondo, quite out of character, was as cool as a cucumber... we were proud of her!

The fateful meeting at the top of the Pass with the Swiss family Guyot was to prove, though we did not know it then, that Switzerland was to become the central factor in our lives, and more so that of Bondo, as she has come to be a permanent resident in that lovely country from which we depart in the Autumn and return to her in the spring. Like migratory birds we go south to the sun while Bondo is left alone to winter in Switzerland.

From Maloja we drove on to the lakeside at Silser-see for the night. We waved to the Swiss family as they passed us in the distance.

About a week later when we came into the camp below the Bernina range we found the Swiss family there. We stayed several days during which time we were invited in for coffee and we reciprocated. This was the beginning of our wonderful friendship with

Denise and Alexandre and their children – Alexandra (fifteen) and Anthony (thirteen). Denise was a dynamic personality in contrast to Alexandre, a softly-spoken, gentle personality whom I would describe as nature's gentleman; only Denise spoke English. She had gone to England just before the outbreak of World War Two to visit her sister who was married to an Englishman. When war broke out she had been unable to return to Switzerland, so she remained throughout the war years, taking a job as companion to a wealthy widow. She remained deeply attached to "my lady" as she referred to her, often returning to England to visit her. Denise was heartbroken when she died only a couple of years ago.

When we parted at the camp they invited us to visit them in Lausanne, which we did a couple of months later. We telephoned when we reached the outskirts of the city for instructions on how to get to them. We became hopelessly lost, finding ourselves on the motorway at the opposite end of the city and had to phone again. They told us to wait where we were and Alexandre came to guide us to their home. Not only did we stay for dinner, but Denise insisted that we stay the night. We protested as we saw that they had only a small two-bedroom flat, but she insisted as it was such a cold night. Anthony was moved into the lounge and Alexandra sent upstairs to share her sister Joumana's tiny flatlet. We were deeply moved by such kindness and hospitality towards utter strangers. This was only the beginning of a sincere friendship of kindness and helpfulness that continues to this day.

From Switzerland we continued on our way to England, where Lynn spent the winter with Bondo in the Somerset home of one of her ex-army friends who had gone on a visit to South Africa. I returned to Israel for the winter. The following spring I returned to join Lynn in England, from where we continued our 'Life with Bondo'. Lynn had investigated the possibility of storing Bondo in Britain during the winters, but found no solution. Bondo's height was against her.

It was only on our way back from Scandinavia towards the end of the summer that we began to worry. Dutch caravanners, whom we met, told us that in Holland caravans are stored in bulb sheds for the winter, but have to be removed in April. Whoever we spoke to regarding storage in Italy threw up their hands in horror – "Nothing would be left," they said, "not even your steering wheel."

Our new Swiss friends had mentioned that they had recently bought a piece of ground near Lake Neuchâtel where they stayed in their trailer caravan when not travelling. Lynn conceived the idea that perhaps we could build a small shed on their land to house Bondo.

So, full speed ahead for Switzerland! On nearing Lausanne we telephoned and were warmly welcomed once again. As they were going to their caravan for the weekend they suggested we join them at the lake. As usual we lost our way! Their 'plot' was on part of a camping holiday village, large enough only to accommodate caravan, car and small garden. Of course, our idea was quite impractical, although they said we were welcome to leave Bondo there during the winter. But Alexandre had a better idea. He went off to the village and returned with the news that he had found a tobacco-drying shed (tobacco is grown in this area) which was not in use and whose owner would be willing to store Bondo every winter. Alexandre undertook to remove the battery and service it for us.

On our return to Switzerland each summer we were met at Lausanne station, taken to their home and next day driven out to the village where Alexandre re-installed our recharged battery and we were 'home'.

Sadly Alexandre died a few years later, just prior to our return to Switzerland – Denise had phoned to break the sad news. A tearful family met us at Lausanne station. We wept with them all the weekend. Anthony bravely carried on his father's kindness towards us – he had prepared our battery and installed it in Bondo, after driving us out to the village.

All the children are now married and have their own children and all live in villages in Canton Vaud. Since her retirement Denise spends all her summers at the holiday village. The year before Alexandre's death they had replaced the caravan with a mobile home (we were there to witness the exchange). With many improvements Denise now has a comfortable lakeside home where she entertains her children and grandchildren.

Bondo in Some of Europe's Capitals

London:

The first year with Bondo we stayed at Cartwright Gardens, which was, in those days, a quiet London suburb, most conveniently situated near Russell Square Underground and Euston station. Surrounding the square were a few very small hotels. We found ourselves parked opposite what turned out to be a hostel for women employees of a London bank. The kind lady in charge invited us to avail ourselves of the facilities of the house, even loaned us a key to enter when the front door was locked after hours. London was ours!

Unfortunately Cartwright Gardens was never the same thereafter. A new hotel opened where the bank hostel had been. Parking meters had been installed all around the square. New developments in the area with consequent population growth had changed the quiet, safe privacy we had then enjoyed.

On our next visit to London we did the conventional thing – we moved into the Caravan Harbour at Crystal Palace. We found it most inconvenient so far from the centre of the city, dependent on public transport. As our main objectives in London are the arts, theatre and ballet, the last act was often spoiled for us as we were always on tenterhooks as to whether or not we would catch that last bus. When we missed it the only bus service in our direction went as far as Brixton, where sometimes there was a connection. Once, when inquiring as to the next connection, the 'clippy' answered most rudely and unsympathetically, "Tomorrow morning!" To find a taxi was not easy, or cheap – and Brixton is no place to run around at that time of night.

One evening when, after a long wait, no buses had appeared going our way, we found that even the Piccadilly Underground station was closed, because the Scottish football team was in London and their fans were so obstreperous that all the bars were also closed against them. To return to camp that night was a nightmare!

The camp anyway was no joy with the over-crowded facilities and general restlessness typical of all camps. We were determined to find other solutions for our next visit to London.

But nothing daunted – we were back in London two years later, determined this time to live in Bondo under more satisfactory conditions, if not in the centre at least close enough to convenient communication facilities.

Whilst visiting friends in the area we discovered that East Finchley station had a very large car park – so we moved in, most convenient, twenty pence only when one drove out. So here we lived happily, even entertaining our friends, to their amusement, at such a convenient address!

When caravanning friends from Kenya, whom we had first met in Norway, came to visit and suggested that we move 'house' to Belsize Park station where they had often stayed, we took their advice as the parking behind that station was more attractive among tall trees and adjoining a tennis club. So once again London was ours, and we expected that from now on would always be so.

Unfortunately, on our next visit, making straight for Belsize Park, we found a barrier across the entrance under which only cars could pass. The authorities had become anti-caravan for obvious reasons! So we returned to East Finchley where we resided satisfactorily for a few days until one evening after our return 'home' the station authorities came up to us suggesting that it would be better if we moved out as a dead body had been found on the edge of the car park just behind us. They offered to guide us to another station car park, but it was too far out so we declined their kind offer.

We paid our twenty pence as we drove out. London at five pence a day – quite a Guinness record, I would say!

*

Paris:

Whenever possible we contrive to arrive in a capital on a Sunday and then it is possible to find parking and enjoy the quieter moments of the metropolis.

Determined to enter Paris early one Sunday morning – Paris was not exactly unknown to us – we reached the outskirts late on Saturday evening after dark and settled down for the night at what we thought was a quiet gateway in the Bois de Vincennes; but what a noisy night. We discovered next morning that we had taken up residence only yards from a busy intersection of about six roads. After that Paris was as quiet as the grave that early Sunday morning.

We stopped on the Place de Bastille for breakfast, Bondo our sidewalk café, so we were able to enjoy watching dancing in the streets by groups of the various Paris departments. It was the weekend before Bastille Day. We lunched on the Ile de la Cité at the edge of the River Seine, opposite the Hôtel de Ville where a band was playing and the music wafted across the River. During the afternoon we also again visited Notre Dame and La Chapelle.

Later we parked on the Rue de Rivoli. On our amble we walked into the Hotel Continental to use their facilities and heard the strains of a wedding march. We dared one another to attend the wedding reception – after all if we are not known to the bride's family we surely are friends of the bridegroom's family and vice versa! So off we rushed to Bondo, unpacked our best Sunday clothes, drew the curtains, attired ourselves, and presented ourselves at the door of the reception hall. When we noticed that invitations were being presented we somehow managed to enter with a group to which, no doubt, we seemed to belong!

Fortunately it was a buffet reception, so we naturally expected to partake of caviar and other French delicacies – but it turned out to be a disappointingly ordinary wedding, and the bride was as ugly as sin and the groom only a little more attractive. We duly helped ourselves to refreshments from the heavily-laden centre table and then approached the bar. The only person at that reception who suspected us of being gatecrashers was the barman who served us double whiskies with a smirk on his face.

We left the reception somewhat inebriated and drove off to hunt for somewhere to spend the night. We crossed the Place de La Concorde and, as it does on most days and nights, La Place resembles a series of race tracks coming from and going in a dozen different directions, at the speed that only Paris traffic knows how. We miraculously emerged with the flow leading to the Rue de Seine running between the river and the park when we suddenly noticed a small road to the right on to which we turned and found ourselves just behind the Petit Palais. There were a few empty parking places. It was like reaching the calm after battling down the rapids. Was it possible we could stay here the night? What could be wrong with the Palais gardens in the very heart of Paris? Judging by the car next to which we drew up no one would disturb us – it was covered with dust and bird droppings and so had obviously been there for some time.

We stepped out to reconnoitre. We could adjust Bondo conveniently over a drain, the solution for our kitchen and bath water. The little road Du Tuit continued on towards the Champs Elysées, but first to the entrance to a driveway – of what? A Daimler or Rolls Royce swung into the driveway at that moment. A smartly uniformed doorman shot out as the car stopped, opened the door with a deep bow and escorted the occupants through the elaborate entrance– Restaurant Le Doyen, Paris' most prestigious! Yes! Le Doyen had what was necessary. Just inside another entrance the cloakroom was most privately situated off a little hall that led to the Bar. The walls were padded with embossed velvet, there were gold taps in the form of horses' heads, the central spout in form unmentionable, high enough above the basin to fill our small water containers. Yes, it would do! And no further away from Bondo than services in a caravan camp. We then proceeded to walk along the avenue of trees running parallel to the Champs Elysées, crossed the wide Rue Winston Churchill to the Grand Palais, and presto, a typical Paris water hydrant for our water supplies, just outside a police station and adjoining the entrance to the Métro. On the other side of the Champs Elysées was the Presidential Palace – a good enough address! Paris was ours. We were 'at home' on Rue Du Tuit for the whole week of Bastille Day celebrations.

When we returned two years later to take up residence again on 'our' Rue Du Tuit, we found other caravans there,

> Hanging out their washing
> On the Champs Elysées.
> No wonder the police,
> A whole squad of them,
> Chased us all away.

It was nearly midnight when we were forced to move on. Attempting to reach the caravan camp in the Bois de Boulogne, we lost our way in the maze of streets that fan out from the Arc de Triomphe. Only in the early hours did we find the Camp, which was so full that dozens of caravans were parked outside the gates. Finally we drove into the empty car park of a nearby restaurant. Exhausted we fell asleep, only to be rudely awakened by loud banging, again by the police – "You have no right on this car park."

We had had enough – we left Paris. The next time that we visited Paris we parked Bondo outside a country railway station and went by train.

*

Brussels:

In Brussels we resided in the vicinity of the Royal Palace and the art galleries – in a comparatively quiet side street.

While there we decided to try to sell our very large antique silver rice spoon as we knew about the famous antique dealers in that city. One of the dealers expressed great interest and offered to come with us to Bondo to inspect the spoon. But once there we could not remember where we had put it. We rummaged and emptied every cupboard in our well appointed caravan with its numerous cupboards–but to no avail. Finally the dealer lost patience and asked us to bring the spoon to him if and when we should find it. He had no sooner left than we remembered that we had not looked in the suitcase under the seat – the dealer had been sitting on that seat! When we brought it to him he made us an offer; his female associate nudged us and suggested we would receive a higher price in London.

When we reached London we attended one of Christie's silver sales and became very excited when we heard the prices that silver items fetched. Their evaluator made a lower offer for ours than we received in Brussels!

In Amsterdam we were advised to take it to Monaco. The spoon is still with us as we have not yet visited Monaco. We were made offers in Copenhagen and Venice, but only for the intrinsic silver value, not its antique value.

I think we will finally present the spoon to our Swiss cousin who is very interested in our family silver.

*

Amsterdam:

We spent our first few nights in Amsterdam on the Singel Canal, with Australian caravanners as neighbours, with whom we became friendly and dined together in a restaurant. Early one morning the police told us to move on. When we told them that we were going on a coach tour of the Hague and Rotterdam they gave us permission to leave Bondo there for the day. On our return in the evening we had no choice but to try and find the caravan camp. We drove and drove, but never reached it. Finally we stopped a taxi and asked the way. The taxi driver replied, "Follow me" – we appreciated his kindness until he charged us the taxi fare to the camp! On the strength of that unwarranted expense we had to forgo the cost of the camp and slept in the avenue outside.

On our 'plot' on another Amsterdam canal behind the Hilton Hotel, we were approached early one morning by one of the nurses from the small, private hospital across the road. We thought she was coming to ask us to move on, but she came with a message from one of the doctors, asking us where he could purchase a caravan like ours. She also told us that the nurses had wanted to offer us coffee when they saw us parked outside the hospital, having taken pity on us gypsies. We greatly appreciated this gesture of hospitality – more than we had had from the daughter of a lifelong friend with a five-storey house who merely gave us dinner and then directed us to this suburban street, after we had told her at dinner that the police had told us that we were not welcome to camp on the Singel Canal.

*

Luxembourg:

We had wandered round Luxembourg after dark looking for somewhere to spend the night. In despair we asked a couple of policemen on patrol where the caravan camp was to be found. Their instructions were so confusing that after a while we gave up looking, and as we so often do in a city, not always with success, made for a group of trees hoping to find a public park, which we did. We cooked and had dinner, but found that the spot was too public as pedestrians passed by every few minutes.

We went for a stroll to hunt a more suitable 'hotel'. Through the trees we saw the lights of a building seemingly set in spacious grounds. On investigation we found its excellent car park – we moved in! It was strange. There were comings and goings all night – lights switching on and off in the building. We could only surmise that maybe it was a maternity hospital and that there must be a population explosion in this mini-state.

After this rather disturbed night I was having my bath when there was a knock on our window. I surreptitiously poked my head out hoping that my nude body was invisible. A voice, in English, asked: "Do you know where you are?" I replied, "Actually no, we have no idea."

"This is Radio Luxembourg," he replied. "And you are occupying space on our car park." I apologised profusely. As soon as we could convert the bathroom we hurriedly drove off. By the light of day we found, just around the corner, a park with gardens and lawns surrounding a large statue of Winston Churchill (just like the one on Westminster Square), so we had breakfast with Winston – pity, we could have slept with him!

Hunting the Loo

Hunting the loo is very much part of 'Life with Bondo,' though she has her own modern 'Porta Potti' which is there in case of need, but we do prefer to find other solutions to that problem.

We discovered, to our amusement, very early on in our travels that there actually exists on the south coast of England a small fishing village by the name of Looe. We have never been able to ascertain whether the common usage of this word has any connection with this village. We have known other references. *Die Kleinhuisie* (Afrikaans) of our childhood days when it was actually a 'little house' standing out of doors. 'The House of the Chair' is the translation from Hebrew – no doubt from some biblical derivation.

It is said that you can judge a nation by its public conveniences and its public gardens. We would put Switzerland at the top of the list, as every car park even has five-star conveniences and France at the bottom in spite of its lovely gardens. But in all fairness we must add that there has been some improvement since the invention of the electronic loo – *la toilette electronique*. To Scotland on the whole one would give higher marks than to England. Yet a stark exception occurred in Somerset: "If one arranges flowers in a church, why not in the loos – it is all part of life." This from the attendant in the municipal toilets in response to our surprised comments. She actually grew the beautiful flowers in her own garden.

In forests we have no alternative but to do as our ancestors did. On occasion, when it is raining, we have used an umbrella, held on high.

In St Moritz we most innocently benefited from our hunt. We had parked at the side of the lake which seemed a most desirable place to settle down for the night, if only we could solve that inevitable problem. There were sports fields in the centre of which was a building, which was apparently the Club House where we would very hopefully be accommodated. Nearby also was an ice-skating rink where an International Competition of 'Ballet on Ice' was in progress. We could hear the music echoing across the fields. We had earlier seen it advertised. We would so love to have watched, but the cost of the tickets was beyond us.

We walked over to the Club House and found that it was closed. Someone obligingly directed us to the ice rink for our purpose. We explained our need at the entrance and were kindly allowed in and directed where to go. Once inside we thought we might just as well stay for the remainder of the performances; so we stood in the passageway between the stands and enjoyed, for the first time, Ice Ballet on international standards. It was worth the cost of the tickets we never bought!

In cities the most obvious solutions are hotels and sometimes restaurants, the larger and the more exclusive the easier it is for us to remain anonymous. This has also offered us the opportunities to become familiar with some of Europe's most famous hotels and restaurants.

In Stockholm we found ourselves excellent parking on the Skeppsholmen, one of Stockholm's many islands of the archipelago, just across the bridge from the National Museum and the Grand Hotel. We had a magnificent view of Gamla (the Old Town), the green copper towers of its famous churches and the Royal Palace reflected in the "silver waters of the Strommen", the same view as described from the front rooms and the breakfast terrace of the Grand.

Because of our regular visits to the sumptuous facilities, the young concierge naturally thought that we were staying at the hotel and treated us with the same respect and courtesy as any other of its distinguished guests. He proffered information about what was on in town, where to find the best restaurants and night clubs as well as where to shop. He even presented us with the Jubilee Brochure of Grand View issued the year before on the Grand's one hundredth birthday (1874–1974) describing it as one of Europe's most élite hotels from which we quote: "During the past century the revolving doors of the Grand have seen a continual stream of princes and diplomats, patrons of the arts and show business, Nobel Prize winners, millionaires and movie stars plus heads of states and guests at royal events." It did not mention the two caravan dwellers on Skeppsholmen Island because we visited a year too late! "The management of the Grand takes on the responsibility of ensuring they take home fond memories of our hospitable international hotel with a Swedish flair." We certainly have fond memories of the Grand. Under these excellent conditions we stayed in Stockholm for twelve days and came to know this beautiful city – Venice of the North.

In Venice, while living on the Lido di Venezia we came to know another of Europe's most exclusive hotels, the Excelsior. Its white, cream and gold interior reflects a sumptuous elegance matched by those other famous Venetian hotels, the Gritti Palace on the Grand Canal or the Danieli.

In Biarritz, on the Atlantic coast of southern France, famous resort of royalty and the rich, the rooms with a view at the Hotel du Palais (once the palace built by Napoleon III for Eugénie, close to her beloved Spain) are among the most expensive in all Europe. We visited this Hotel du Palais to use their facilities and even the writing room, sending greetings on the hotel note paper to impress our friends. Bondo stood in the hotel driveway among the Rolls Royces.

In Amsterdam we parked on the Singel Canal, a comfortable distance from that famous restaurant Die Port van Cleve. One of the hallmarks of Amsterdam, opening in 1870 as the Niewe Bierhaus, it has been a favourite haunt of journalists and politicians to this day. The restaurant is renowned for its numbered steaks. Its beefsteaks are a 'statistical dish'. The tally when we were in Amsterdam was approaching five million. When a customer orders a steak he receives a card with his number on it.

In his 'Holidays in Holland', BBC programmer Michael Barsley (reporter, author and producer) recorded his visit to this famous restaurant. His steak number was 4,610,770. And Sidney Clark in his book *All the Best in Holland* describes the restaurant in some detail. He did not however describe that part which was familiar to us.

In appreciation we wrote to the management as follows:

The Management
Die Port van Cleve

Dear Sirs,
Neither Michael Barsley of the BBC nor Sidney Clark in his book All the Best in Holland, *when speaking and writing about Die Port van Cleve, mentioned the special hospitality which we will always remember and deeply*

appreciated as caravan globe-trotters who were unable
to afford your famous numbered 'biefstuk' and
regretfully are unable to add another number.

   But thank you for the petunia-pink basins and bowls
with black seats and the marble walls.

          Yours faithfully
          The occupants of the caravan on the Singel Canal

We had hoped that as a result of this letter and in appreciation of our little joke the manager would invite us to partake of a numbered steak on our next visit to the petunia-pink facility. We would never know, because another visit was denied us, as the next day we were informed by the police that "the Singel Canal was not a caravan park" and politely asked to move on.

With Bondo in Norway

Our Welcome to Norway

We set forth from Newcastle on the afternoon of June 25th, on the car ferry *Jupiter* of Bergen Lines, on our first great Scandinavian adventure, arriving at Stavanger early next morning. We were disappointed at first at our introduction to the "Land of the Midnight Sun" as it was raining and misty.

The ship glided slowly through the mist and drizzle, interspersed with heavy downpours which drove us from the decks. Was it the mainland on our right or were we sailing between islands – were we entering a fjord? It was puzzling and mysterious and exciting.

The land consisted of low rocky hills covered with small trees and bushes. Colourfully painted wooden cottages with unfamiliar roof pitches were set among the hills or at the water's edge. Innumerable craft, large and small in many bright colours, were anchored in the grey rock coves or moving gracefully across the still water.

This was a strange new world, dreamlike in its simple beauty, unlike anything we had ever seen. We already knew then that we would love Norway.

We docked at Bergen at about half past three in the afternoon. We drove along the seafront past the famous old houses at Bryggen, past the fish market and into the main square, unaware that it was the Town Centre, a peaceful 'lounge' where traffic was prohibited. We stopped next to the Torvalmenningen monument. We had no sooner stopped when suddenly a screaming man threw himself to the ground – a white-coated man, whom seconds before I had seen putting on the white coat, went up to him, felt his pulse and opened his collar. I thought he was either a drug addict or an epileptic as he lay there screaming and kicking, and so the inevitable crowd gathered. Suddenly he got up, whereupon the white-coated man started to make a speech. The 'epileptic' then started handing out pamphlets, well-illustrated with cartoons, which of course we could not understand, but presumably political. Police appeared and just stood around and spoke to them. What a clever way to rustle up an audience! We then approached one of the policemen and asked permission to park there while we went to the tourist office to obtain literature and maps. He graciously assented.

When we emerged from the tourist office armed with maps, a small booklet, *Norway in a Nutshell,* and their very excellent and most informative literature which is published for visitors to Norway, a youth band was marching down the street, the young drum major swinging her baton, throwing it into the air and skilfully catching it. The blond, blue-eyed lovely children were dressed in attractive brown and white uniforms. We were told that it was the Oslo contingent that had just arrived. The atmosphere was gay with everyone enthusiastically clapping them as they passed. During the following days we were to enjoy the other groups, each in different gaily coloured uniforms, performing in the park.

We drove off and quite by chance found parking in a quiet street between public buildings and a flower-filled park. Unfortunately it was meter parking, and as I went to insert my coins a policeman came up and stopped me. "Visitors do not have to pay, only the locals – welcome to Bergen." I asked if we could stay on. His reply: "As long as you wish." So we were 'at home' in Bergen. The public building opposite us was an extension of the museum with a small concert hall where Grieg concerts are held from time to time which we were able to attend.

Our 'garden' had such beautiful flowers!

*

Going Fishing

We left Bondo outside the shop on the main road at Hovland, on the Sorfjord, as the road down into the village was very steep and we saw no possibility of a level parking place – something we always had to look for. We walked down towards the wharf, first passing a factory which subsequently turned out to be a spinning mill.

At the wharf were two men preparing to go out to set their fishing nets. They had a large boat with motor and cabin and a tall mast for a sail. Their reaction to our interest was an invitation to go out with them in the boat – it was so spontaneous. With them was a fourteen-year-old boy with blond hair below his shoulders shivering from his swim in the icy water. He spoke fluent English. In reply to our question how come he spoke such excellent English he told us that he had a good teacher who had spent two years in England. Otta had been learning the language for three years, a very bright boy with a girlish face. Otta climbed the mast to show off his masculinity. He did not accompany us. We set off at about eight in the evening, Olav navigating. The younger man, Knut, about forty years old, let the brand new green nylon net out so fast that he lost the end, probably because the boat was moving too fast He said this was the first time such a thing had happened to him with a fishing net. Olav then slowed down the motor and turned around so that Knut could retrieve the net.

It was a wonderful sensation drifting in the middle of the fjord on the still, pink sunset-lit water with the dark reflections of the mountains on either side. On one side the mountain sloped down to a shelf of pale green fields and orchards at the water's edge. On the other side of the fjord the mountain rose sharply and much higher to the white of the Folgefonn, the third largest glacier in Norway. White-streaked reflections broke through the dark reflection on the water below. Above us the sky was clear and cloudless. "This summer is the driest since 1959," Olav remarked. Several days before, we had tried, unsuccessfully, from Jondal on the other side of the Folgefonn, to reach a tongue of the glacier by driving as far as passable on a very rough road and then walking and climbing over very rough terrain, at times boggy, at times rocky.

We drifted in the middle of the Sorfjord for about two hours and had very interesting conversations with Olav and Knut who both spoke reasonably good English. They told us two legends: there had been settlements on top of the mountains above the Hardanger many thousands of years ago, but the people were bad. One day a young girl came down to the fjord and when she went back she found that her village had disappeared under twenty feet of ice and snow. Confirmation of this story was evidenced by utensils, etc., that were washed down from the plateau by rivers.

The second legend: Olav pointed to some snow on the mountain above Hovland and said that when the snows melted, leaving a patch the size and shape of a cow it was time to send the cattle up for summer grazing.

Olav told us that he was born on an island on the Hardanger, his father had married a woman from the Sorfjord. He was a bachelor and lived with his mother and father. Otta, the fourteen-year old, was his nephew. I think they all lived in the big house by the wharf. Olav, now working at the spinning mill, had been to sea – Caribbean, Pacific, Red Sea and Gulf of Akaba. He has just spent Kr. 12,000 on the new cabin for this fishing boat which he built himself. It was very smart with a floral fawn wall to wall (port to starboard is more correct) carpet. Below the hatches were two bunks for sleeping. He said the boat was seaworthy for the North Sea in summer.

I was interested to learn what happened here during World War II. I gathered that Olav was in the Resistance. He told how the allies dropped guns and ammunition on to the top of the mountain and the Germans, on finding out about the drop, gave an ultimatum that if they did not give up the ammunition they, the Germans, would take away their women and children. On another occasion when the fjord froze the Germans dynamited the ice in order to pass through with a boat. The water again froze trapping the boat and the Norwegians killed them. When the British came in 1945 they were joined by the Norwegians who hung their German prisoners on trees, so did not waste valuable ammunition by shooting them.

Knut had worked at Spitzbergen in the coal mines. At Odda, a few miles from here, at the end of the fjord, are large aluminium works. They also told us that the Germans destroyed everything north of Narvik. Actually they over-ran the whole of Norway and did terrible deeds. Today most tourists are Germans...

Although taxes are high in Norway the standard of living is also high. They had been to Majorca on holiday paid for by the spinning mill – they only had to pay for their beers. They laughingly said that they were hungry in Majorca as Norwegians are used to big meals at home. Knut lives with his seventy-four-year-old father who still cuts hay. A neighbour, at the age of ninety-four, also still cuts hay.

They informed us that the cattle population had been cut by forty per cent and as a result of more intensive feeding milk production had increased by thirteen per cent. In this area cattle farming had been abandoned as fruit farming is more profitable – strawberries, cherries, apples, pears, and also potatoes, as part of their staple diet, are grown. Fruit canning is an extensive industry. At Loftus we later visited an experimental fruit farm – we had never before seen such wonderful cherries!

It was lovely out on the fjord – we so enjoyed the conversations with our hosts and were sorry when the trip came to an end. Knut had to go on duty on his motor bike, so Olav took us to visit the spinning mill. There were the most wonderful varieties of colours and Olav told us that they mix cotton and nylon thread with the wool. It was lovely and soft to the touch. This was Friday evening and the factory was in full swing.

After visiting the factory we decided to drive back a short distance along the road to a lay-by we had seen earlier. It was already very late, about 11 p.m. So here we slept on the very edge of the fjord surrounded by beautiful birch trees, whose silver barks glistened in the moonlight. We stayed here all the next day watching the changing clouds and colours and reflections across the fjord.

At about lunch-time, Otta, the fourteen year old, arrived on his bicycle – he was delivering newspapers. He stayed to lunch with us on smoked mackerel. A very bright kid and generally knowledgeable and of course so fluent in English. He goes to school at Kinsarvik, eight kilometres away and finds the bus journey there and back rather a nuisance. Said he wants to go to sea when he finishes school. In the afternoon he came again, this time across the bay in his father's rowing boat.

We again stayed the night. We saw the dawn at midnight and again at 3 a.m. This was really a lovely 'camp' on this narrow fjord between high mountains and the glacier opposite.

*

At Home with Vigeland

In Oslo we found a satisfactory site, with all conveniences, in the Frognor Park, adjoining the Vigeland Sculpture Gardens and Museum, where we were able to live with the works of this famous Norwegian sculptor – they are all there – the granite figures spiralling the huge obelisk and the massive granite groups of figures projecting downwards from the obelisk. The other outstanding sculpture is the fountain, its basin supported by bronze figures, and the pool below surrounded by bronzes depicting the life cycle from childhood to old age.

One very hot morning, while we were enjoying the sculptures in the Park, we saw the loveliest sight – a sight which would have given Gustav Vigeland, so adept at sculpturing babies and children, such joy to see his sculptures come to life – a kindergarten class of naked toddlers splashing in the pool around his famous fountain. Also in the Vigeland Gardens are beautiful bronzes, singly and in pairs, lining both sides of the wide bridge across the lake.

During our stay we had the pleasure of attending a chamber concert in the courtyard of the Vigeland Museum, which was formerly Vigeland's home and studio and now houses thousands of his works, making it possible to follow some of his works from the very first pencil line sketches and models to the finished work. Several years later, we also visited Mandel, his birth-place in southern Norway.

*

Over the Top and Down Again

Bondo affords us the possibility of living in and with the extravaganza of nature which is Norway, and freedom to move house from one magnificent area to another, to stay or to move on according to our will and the weather, by the light of day and of night.

We live freely on the shores of the fjords and lakes, fast-flowing rivers; opposite roaring cascades and waterfalls dropping down from the mountains above us, the glaciers bright in the midday sun, pale translucent pink at midnight and orange at dawn.

One afternoon we drove up from the end of the Luster Fjord, a finger of the Sognefjord, the longest in Norway stretching 112 miles inland from the sea. In the valley at the end of the fjord whole families, even the smallest children were working in the hayfields – blond-haired, blue-eyed, sturdy, good-looking people always with a ready smile as they waved to us as we passed by.

The road climbed steadily upwards through lovely forests of birch trees with their gleaming silver barks until we reached a bleak landscape above the tree line. There was no indication on our map that we would be climbing. Suddenly a heavy mist enveloped us. We climbed steadily on, the mist swirling around us. We did not see, until

we were almost on it, a signboard reading 1,440 METRES ABOVE SEA
LEVEL. When the mist lifted we found ourselves in an Arctic world. It
was bitterly cold.

As it was already late we had no alternative but to find a level
parking to spend the night. We prepared ourselves hot soup and tucked
ourselves up in bed with hot water-bottles. The mystic white light on
the snow was a little weird and almost frighteningly lonely. We slept
fitfully.

The next morning we awoke to sunshine and blue skies. We were
certainly in a beautiful world of snow, ice and water. There were little
lakes with detached ice floes floating on them and in places the road
passed between three-metre high snow banks tinted pink by a type of
algae.

We studied our maps more carefully. We were on the Jotunheimen
Plateau.

From this lonely world of ice and snow and distant white peaks we
descended once again through birch forests until we reached the lush
valley of Boverdalon with a wide river flowing in and out of small
lakes.

There were farms with fertile fields, busy farmers and grazing
cattle. Then on to the little town of Lom where we stayed for some
days. Here we witnessed a wedding procession on its way to the
ancient, restored, stave church (the original church was first
mentioned in 1270, but thought to be much older). A fiddler led the
colourful procession followed by the bride and groom in traditional
costumes – the bride resplendent with an elaborate head-dress. They
were followed by a retinue of children and guests all in national
costumes. From Lom we planned to visit the famous Gieranger fjord,
but this time we first studied a topographical map and consequently
decided to leave Bondo in Lom and travel by bus and book ourselves
into a room for an overnight stay.

How right we were. The road rose steeply to a great height, once
again into a white world of frozen lakes and snow-covered mountain
ranges. Then descending into the deep cleft in the mountain down
innumerable hairpin bends to the water level of that most spectacular
of Norway's fjords with its mighty walls rising sheer from the water
and so many water-falls tumbling down from the heights above.
Nature's extravaganza indeed.

It was certainly Over the Top and Down again!

Criss-Crossing France

Bondo always behaves crossing France from east to west as she is then on the home stretch because she was born in the UK and still retains citizenship. We have crossed France with Bondo from Switzerland to La Manche several times and from north to south as many times, thereby getting to know a large part of that country; we have passed so close to areas through which we passed before without really being aware. There is a repeat of the great rivers, the woodlands, the farms, the canals – but the towns all have their own characters and so do the villages. There are many villages that stand out in our memories, especially the flower-bedecked ones. We have also visited friends and made new friends in France. We have had good experiences and unpleasant experiences – but mostly good.

Perhaps we should pause in Folkestone where there is a memorial to all the men of two World Wars, "Who passed this way to France."

Travelling through this vast country we keep asking ourselves how it was possible for Hitler's armies to sweep through and occupy it in such a short space of time. A feature of French towns and villages is that every one of them has war memorials to their dead of two World Wars as well as to those who fell in earlier wars throughout the centuries. And among the recent memorials are also a few memorialising civilians and maquis who were taken away by the Germans during World War Two – usually only a few names, also the few Jews.

We have visited the great cathedral cities of Rouen, Rheims, Orléans, Bourges, Metz where we visited their cathedrals and marvelled at their intricate facades, stained glass windows, great gothic pillars, their altars and their vastness.

We have stayed at Avallon, Vezelay, Laon, all three with their fine churches; Arles, made famous by Van Gogh, where we witnessed a bullfight and were there for a festival of parades and folk-dancing in

Sixt L'Abbaye – Val de Giffre, Savoie, France

the Roman arena; Aix-en-Provence, the home of Cézanne, from where we saw the view from his window which he often painted. Here we also enjoyed '*musique dans les rues*' and especially memorable, a harp and flute concert in the convent courtyard; Beziers with its most beautiful park; Montpellier; Pau from where one obtained a panoramic view of the Pyrenees; Biarritz; Bayonne; Saintes and its Roman ruins; Niort, that flower-bedecked town; Abbaye Fontrevaud where we visited the tombs of Henry II and his queen and slept nearby beside a little lake; Montserau, where we met and were entertained by a well-known local artist; spent many days visiting the Châteaux of the Loire; beautiful Besançon, its two rivers and university and renowned early clock; Annecy on its canals and lovely lake; Chambéry and its statue of huge elephants; Grenoble, university and industrial city; Chartreuse Monastery.

We have also been to the beautiful areas of the French Alps, Route Napoleon, the Cevennes, the Languedoc; the source of the Loire with friends who live in the area; the Bordeaux forest; the Morvan whose hills are the sources of several rivers, and La Route des Dauphins etc.

Bondo has steered us through country undulating with fields of many colours and ploughed lands of deep rich soil broken by groups of thick forest areas, remains of primeval forests which once covered Europe. A glorious afternoon of vivid colours, the patchwork of purple lavender and ripening golden wheat, an expanse of pale mauve poppies (will they yield *opium*?); large herds of white cows and sheep and an old woman driving a cow; fields of maize and oats and barley; fields of lucerne and fields of cabbages and hothouses covering acres of long cucumbers from which a kindly farmer gave us one. Harvesters and balers – farm buildings, some surrounding a courtyard, others L-shaped – in Normandy the half-timbered and thatched buildings – houses with French windows leading out of each room and raised above the wine cellars. Suddenly we see a castle, Mont Sabot on top of a small hill. Wide open vistas above a spacious valley – patchwork of forest and fields, fields divided by hedgerows, virginia creepers in autumn colours climbing a cottage wall – dark and white clouds overhead and then the most beautiful sunset just before reaching Arnay-le-Duc – a bright orange-red sky and clouds of pink hanging in the sky, and to the east mauve and purple cloud effects.

After that gorgeous sunset, marred by being on a main road with very heavy traffic, we came to Arnay-le-Duc, described in the guidebook in one line: "A picturesque little town with its pretty Promenade de l'Arquebuse." We did not see the "pretty promenade" as we arrived after dark into a town with very narrow streets, deafened by the *camions* passing through one after the other. We do not know how people can live in this "picturesque little town" with so much noise of traffic. We parked beside a stream hoping to spend the night here as it was quiet, but the stream stank – so we had to find a way to get out of the town on to the route we wanted. We went into a pub and were told to take the road marked Lyons – we were on the main road to Lyons, hence the heavy traffic – but told that about two kilometres along this road we would find a signpost to Beaune. So off we drove and turned off as directed and found ourselves in Suivry and had a marvellous quiet night on a lay-by near a Relais lorry park and restaurant.

We drove off from Suivry in the morning after being greeted by white cows. We came to a road leading to the source of the river Ouche through beautiful hilly country to a valley of vines after descending a short tree-lined avenue. The next village was Bouze-les-Beaune, an apt name as we were in the wine district of Burgundy, which became merged into the French Province in 1477.

Bondo and ourselves merged with the French Provinces in the twentieth century.

Rochefort village on La Route des Dauphins

Scottish Saga

We set out for Torridon, a wonderful drive at the foot of the Damh range at the edge of the upper Torridon loch, then crossed a bridge over a fast-running river which came from a wide open glen and ran into the loch.

We reached the Visitors' Centre to learn that this vast Nature Reserve was the property of the Scottish National Trust We collected pamphlets giving detailed information on the area. They advised us to do the classic walk between the mountains, which started from the climbers' car park. This seemed a good idea, so we drove off down a steep narrow secondary road for about two-and-a-half miles, partly through a beautiful forest of Scots pine, crossed a stone bridge over a deep gorge with a lovely waterfall and arrived at the parking lot – a large tarmac area at the riverside, surrounded by a forest of pine and rhododendron and above us the Ben Alligan giants (or monroes, as Scottish peaks over three thousand feet above sea level are referred to).

Here we slept our first night on what we came to refer to as "our Rhododendron Park". At night we were alone on the car park. The next day we decided to try the recommended walk, but not to walk the eight hours to the Visitors' Centre which was too far, but to go part of the way and return the same way.

We started off through part of the Torridon Forest along the river which cascaded down a deep gorge. The sound of rushing water filled the air. We followed the course of the river. On either side of us the U-shaped glacial valley swept steeply upwards from the valley floor, the river being the lowest point. The peaks on our left were all over three thousand feet. At this point we were still unfamiliar with the names. We were fascinated by the deep gash in the high peak and the three rugged peaks of the same range.

The Church and the Manse on Loch Torridon

It was a lovely hot day and I was tempted to slip off my clothes and cool off in the river – a little risky as we were in view of the path, though we had met only one party of walkers all morning. Lynn kept cave. It was well worth the chance – the water was icy, but very refreshing. Nobody came by. A little further beyond we came to a waterfall falling into a deep gorge with perpendicular wall-like sides. We continued up the river, criss-crossing several times with great difficulty over stepping stones in the fast-moving stream. The sky was clear but heat-hazy. We rested in the shade of overhanging banks at the side of the river.

Then we went on climbing out of the lowest part of the valley towards the high mountain. It was very hot. To cool down we lay in the shade of a large rock and actually had a twenty-minute sleep. Refreshed, we made for a higher ridge towards another stream cascading down from the mountain above. The going was rough, but we were enjoying ourselves – we wondered whether we could tackle some of the higher climbs. The valley and the mountains were now very lovely in the early evening light. We climbed down towards our Rhododendron Park, reaching 'home' at about eight o'clock. Once again all the climbers' cars had gone and we were alone. After a good supper we had an excellent night, healthily tired from the day's effort. It had been a wonderful day.

The next day we decided to explore the area below us. After passing through a small gate through a tunnel of rhododendron bushes, a side path led to the edge of a tiny lochan with a rhododendron island in the middle, reflecting its colours into the water among masses of water-lilies. At the edge of the opposite bank was a wall of rhododendron backed by dark Scots pines.

Following the path in the direction of Loch Torridon we came out on a terrace and there below, on a small hillock stood a small church silhouetted against the loch. Some yards beyond and below the slope was the Manse. We visited the church – not old, of very simple rough stone exterior and interior and beautiful open beamed roof. What type of vicar ministered these tiny villages of Torridon, Alligan and Diabaig? We were curious – how could we go about meeting him? We visualised a little wizened old Scotsman, perhaps an eccentric on his last job before retirement. Perhaps if we told him that we came from the Holy Land and were regular guests at the Church of Scotland

Hospice in Tiberias and St Andrews Scotch Hospice in Jerusalem we could use this as an introduction.

We proceeded in the direction of the small, white double-storied house surrounded by a tall hedge. As we approached a large black dog came out of the house, gave a friendly bark and came towards us wagging his tail. We were taken aback when a tall young man in sports outfit followed. Rather shyly he invited us in – no need to use our introduction!

The front room, into which he led us, was scattered with books on the shelves and tables and on the floor, obviously a bachelor's establishment. The large black dog and black cat completed the family. He introduced himself as Peter and we likewise used only our first names. It appears that he had spent some years in Zambia serving on a mission station, so of course there was much to talk about. Lynn had lived in Zambia for a number of years. He had great respect for and love of the African peoples. We discussed books on Africa – he had read all those we had read and recommended some others.

Tea was offered and served rather awkwardly. He told us how he loved the mountains of Scotland and had been happy to accept this parish which afforded him the chance to live among them and climb during his free time. The mountains were almost a passion with him. We learnt from him the names of all the peaks in the area and that he had climbed every one of them. He said that when the weather was fine he often went up with his dog and stayed all night – enjoying the sunset, the moonlight and the dawn. He felt that he knew every stone on these mountains and promised to show us some of the many slides he had taken. We left at about five o'clock after Peter had accepted our invitation to dinner the following evening.

Instead of going 'home' the way we had come we decided to climb up towards the mountain. There was no path, the grass was thick and matted, the heather harsh and scratchy but, a joy to note, it was coming into bloom. We had to avoid the boggy patches where hidden springs ran below the spongy softness of thick moss, a conglomerate of minute tightly impacted flowers in green and maroon. We clambered up over the pink and grey boulders characteristic of the Torridon area, geologically known as Torridon Rock made up of very ancient Lewisian gneiss.

Looking up it seemed impossible for us to climb higher, but looking down we were amazed to see how far we had already come.

The church and the manse looked like tiny toys on the edge of the great Torridon loch, backed by high mountains and every inlet and peninsula visible like a great map spread out below us. A grey haziness indicated the invisible sea beyond.

We came to a spring with a trickle of water dripping over a rock shelf like a miniature waterfall. We drank from it and were refreshed. We made for the ridge above us – that would be our maximum capacity, so we thought. But when we reached that ridge there was yet another and still no view of the high mountains beyond. Having come so far we decided to climb on. It seemed the most important thing in the world to reach the point where we could obtain a clear view of Beinn Alligin and its highest crag Sgur Mohr (3,232 ft). We puffed and panted, climbing steeply towards the saddle or 'corrie' as it is called in Scotland, relieved at last to climb over the ridge and out of its shadow into the sun. Before us lay an almost level plateau made up of areas of both flat rock and massive boulders. The great summits towered above. We sat down on a rock to rest. Suddenly – I saw, on a wide grassy corrie above us, seven to eight deer. I pointed, too excited to speak. When they realised we had seen them they started to move off, for a moment hidden behind a rise, then emerging as they walked on while the stag stood still watching us and covering their retreat. Through the field glasses I could clearly see his beautiful antlers. It was obvious that they had been watching us before we saw them. From where we now were we had a magnificent view of the giant peaks and the sweep of the valley below.

The climb down was steep and at times we had to manoeuvre our way between the boulders to avoid the marshy ground, using the thick tufts of grass as steps.

The sun was now setting in a hazy pink. Far below we could see the tiny square of the car park with Bondo a lonely speck on it. It took us an hour from the start of our descent when we finally reached 'home' well after 9 p.m. We prepared our meal, for it was many hours since we had last eaten, and we had certainly expended much energy. We were soon in bed. Tomorrow we would have to go to the village to shop for the dinner party that evening with our new friend.

At 7.15 on the dot Peter arrived dressed in his black clerical clothes. He explained that he had come direct from officiating at a funeral.

The dinner was a great success. We served:

Cockaleekie Soup (Baxter's famous)
Hot Sheeps' Tongues
Potatoes, Peas and Salad
Pineapple Rings & Cream for dessert
Ginger Beer, being the beverage
(Peter, of course, being teetotal)

Discussion covered a wide range of subjects. He knew very little about Israel and asked many questions. When we spoke of our visits to the Sinai his interest was aroused, it seems more about climbing Mount Sinai and Mount Sobol than its biblical and religious significance.

It was nearly midnight when he left. He invited us to his church for the Holy Communion service next morning.

I was amazed how the ancient custom of Christ's day and our present day custom of the thanksgiving blessing over wine, the fruit of the vine and bread, the fruit of the earth, had been incorporated into Christianity with an entirely different connotation.

The next morning we decided to attempt to climb the mountain with its strange cleft, the Sgur Mhor (The Axe). We thought that if we followed the path it may lead us in the right direction for the ascent. (Paths in Scotland are, on the whole, very poorly marked and generally in poor condition). Lynn does not like paths, she considers them restricting and so she headed directly up the steep slope. I am more conservative and perhaps less foolhardy. I like to follow a path. Lynn was soon out of sight – this was no way to behave on the mountain and I was furious. I followed, shouting into the emptiness. I finally caught up with her and we continued in the direction towards the mountain. Eventually we found ourselves in an area of massed giant rocks, a dump of boulders below the Sgur Mhor, the result of a great landslide (we later read) which formed the deep cleft which reaches to the summit. Certainly there was no way we could proceed any further, but it was interesting to see this strange mountain at close quarters.

On the way down we found a path which no doubt circumvented the mountain for a possible ascent. It was now too late in the day to attempt the climb to the top, so we followed the path downwards which obviously led back to the car park. Lynn, now on the path, caught her foot in a hole and fell forward on her face hitting her upper forehead on a protruding stone, fortunately not a jagged one. She was bleeding profusely but managed the half-hour walk to our caravan. After some perfunctory first-aid we drove off to Torridon to find a doctor. We were directed to the locum as the local doctor was on leave. He put a plaster along the still bleeding wound and advised us to proceed immediately to Inverness to the hospital there – some eighty-five miles away, usually a three-day journey for us. He gave us a letter, quote – *"Dear doctor... I think a stitch would be wise if you agree."* We were very upset, at best it would be three to four hours drive arriving at the hospital about midnight. We stopped at the village of Kinlochewe some ten miles on to fill up with petrol. We asked the petrol attendant whether there was a doctor at Kinlochewe. "Who needs a doctor?" he replied. "You go and see our Sister Brown, sure she will help you." He directed us to her house at the edge of the village. She bathed and dressed the wound, pressed the skin well together and put on a plaster at right angles to the cut, not along it! No need for stitches. What a kind, sweet woman she was.

By now it was quite dark so we drove out of the village and parked for the night in a clearing at the side of the road, feeling quite confident that all was well.

The next morning Sister Brown, passing along the road on her rounds, saw us and called in to see her patient. She asked us where she could find us next day as she would like to examine the wound and re-dress it. When we suggested the Climbers' Car Park she said it would be convenient, as she would be passing there anyway. On the way back through Torridon we met our vicar and he invited us to tea and to see his slides. Lynn was feeling okay, so we accepted.

In the late afternoon we made our way down the slope from "Rhododendron Park" where Peter was waiting for us on the road and drove us in his little car at great speed along the rough dirt road to his house where we were greeted enthusiastically by the black dog and cat.

It was a gorgeous evening. Small flecks of clouds tinted pink by the setting sun changed continually in shape and form. The loch was very still, reflecting the mountains opposite, Beinn Damh sweeping up like an enormous cone and beside it the saucer-shaped summit. We have seen the same formation in Norway and Switzerland which there hold glaciers. The sharp, long shadows of the peaks dramatised their forms. We could well understand how Peter loved his mountains and the reason why so young a man was prepared to serve so small and dwindling a parish. He had been in Torridon for four years living alone beside the loch. We spent the evening viewing his magnificent slides of the area, many of them taken from the summits of the highest peaks. For us it was a wonderful addition to our stay in the area and encouraged us to try for the summits. When we left it was still light with a pinkish haze. Peter said he had never known such a sky.

The next day at about noon Sister Brown arrived to dress Lynn's wound. She worked with such gentleness, concern and expertise, dedicated in every action. She was on her way to Diabaig and invited us to go with her. She drove her small car with as much expertise as she dressed wounds. She told us that she had been working in the area for twenty-five years in the days when the road was merely a rough track. We were told later that during the worst storms and snow she never failed to be where she was needed. A kind, unassuming and modest little woman. Twenty years on we still exchange Christmas Greetings and Calendars and have even visited her since then, now retired and living on the shore of Loch Torridon.

Diabaig is at the end of the Torridon peninsula, at one time no doubt an important fishing village. Now there remain only a few fishermen and a few crofters. The road descends to the few scattered houses at a 1:3 gradient. Peter had told us of an Edinburgh architect and his wife who had 'escaped' to the country and were becoming crofters and were building their house themselves at Diabaig. We met him and I told him that we knew about him. He invited us into the caravan they were living in temporarily. We joined them for tea and oatcakes. In his childhood they were neighbours of friends of ours in Edinburgh. She had just come in from tending the sheep. They admitted that life was fairly tough on this windswept headland. They overlook a deep bay with wild rough-and-tumble gneiss rock hills dipping down into the sea – the roughest landscape we have ever seen. We climbed above the house and looked across the sea to Skye and the Hebrides in the far distance which were visible as it was such a clear day. We passed the post office, the smallest in Great Britain.

*

A Day of Accomplishment and Wonder that Ended in an Encounter with Tragedy

The next day again a glorious, clear summer's day. We set off by following the path which ascended the three ridges which we had climbed the previous Friday and where we had seen the deer. We reached the coire following the stream that came down the mountain. It was quite hard going but we tried to keep on the springy moss underfoot, sometimes finding ourselves in bogs, at other times among rocks. There was a great feeling of loneliness with the mountains towering above.

Before tackling the really steep part we stopped to have our lunch of sandwiches and fruit. During this stop we met the first people – a middle-aged couple with a young girl and a dog. We had earlier seen a young man ahead of us. The only other encounters were with ptarmigans and the ever present sheep.

We finally reached the shoulder of the coire between Meall an Laoigh translated Calf Mound, and Tom na Gruagaich, the Knoll of the Damsel. We then climbed to the Peak of the Damsel (3,029 ft) on which stood a stone beacon. From here we had superb views all around. To the west the Isle of Skye and the Hebrides, to the south Loch Torridon and the Applecross range comprising Beinn Damh, Loch Damh and Beinn Shieldaig; to the east Beinn Dearg and Beinn Eighe and range upon range beyond and just north-east of us the immediate ridge of Squr and to the north-west more ranges as far as Cape Wrath, the most northerly point of north-west Scotland.

The air was clear and balmy. The family with the dog had already gone on to Squr Mhor and we could see that it was a long hard climb. Later three young people came down from Squr Mhor and the young girl and one of the men complained that it had been a hard climb, and we think that decided us not to tackle it, but instead to climb Meall an Laoigh. We were recompensed by the wonderful rock formation up there – layer upon layer of flat compressed rock and the views of Loch Torridon and Diabaig at the end of Loch Torridon.

After spending a couple of hours on the peaks we set off down the same route. On our right the steep cliff of Meall an Laoigh threw a shadow by the setting sun and we finally reached the bottom at 8 p.m.

As we approached our Rhododendron Park we saw a car with a boat on top with only Bondo as its companion, as all the other cars had already departed, their owners having come down the mountain before us. A woman stepped out of the car asking if we had seen her husband and son who had left at 2 p.m. to cross all the ridges of the range. Our reply was that they could not possibly be down before 9 p.m. as the full climb by experienced mountain walkers takes fully seven hours, so we invited her for tea while she waits. She and husband and twenty-three-year-old son were camping near the Visitors' Centre in the woods where we had lunched the week before and where we nearly turned Bondo over trying to park on very rough ground.

At nine o'clock their son, Simon, arrived and was shocked to find that his father was not already there. He said that they had had an argument as to which was the shortest climb down and each had decided to go their own way. Simon wanted to go back to look for his father but his mother refused to let him go alone. We immediately suggested that Peter, with his knowledge of the mountains, would be the right person to accompany Simon on his search.

So while Lynn and Simon prepared blankets, a hot flask and brandy, Mary and I went off in her car to fetch Peter. When we arrived at his house it was in darkness, the dog barked and therefore I presumed that Peter was at home, as he had told us that the dog always accompanied him. We rang the front doorbell over and over again, there was no response. We shouted and still no response. I then suggested that we throw gravel up against the upstairs windows accompanied by shouting in case he was asleep. Again no response after again and again ringing the bell and shouting. By this time we could only conclude that he had gone out without the dog.

We drove back to Torridon and there raised the alarm. A representative of the Mountain Rescue Team met us and told us that they would not be able to organise a search until first light. He suggested that Simon and his mother spend the night at the inn and Simon could go up with the Rescue Team in the morning.

We woke before 5 a.m. It was already quite light. At 4.55 a police car arrived at the car park followed by about six cars and a pale blue police van, also Simon and Mary in their car with a boat on top. What I thought was Peter's car also arrived but he did not get out of it. It was about 5.15 a.m. when they all drove off towards Alligin.

We stopped the postman at 10.30 a.m. and he gave us the terrible news that the man's body had been found. When Simon came back later he told us that his father had fallen over a cliff and broken his neck and had presumably died instantly. He advised us to move on. We also felt that we did not want to stay there any longer.

We waited in Torridon to offer our condolences to Mary. Peter had been sent for and was with her. He was terribly upset that we had failed to wake him – of course he would have gone with Simon. He had been up on the mountain the whole day and the night before because the weather was so marvellous and had slept so heavily on his return home that he had not heard us. How tragic. We had been with Mary and Simon in their most tragic hours and our friendship with them has lasted all these many years.

Simon blamed himself for parting from his father on the mountain and could find no peace. That next autumn he climbed alone in the Scottish mountains deliberately endangering himself. He was found in a serious state of exposure.

Soon after he decided to join the British army. When the army organised an expedition to climb in the Himalayas he begged to be included.

For the final assault to the heights Simon was not considered to be a sufficiently experienced mountaineer, so he remained at the upper base camp. One of the climbers fell and was seriously injured. When members returned to the upper base camp to organise the rescue Simon volunteered to climb up and stay with and tend the injured climber. By so doing he saved his life.

Strangely, that night he spent with the injured climber on the mountain was the anniversary of his father's death on Beinn Alligin.

Now, after all these years of close friendship with the family, staying often in Mary's home when she would drive us around her home counties of the Cotswolds that she loved so well; or she would join us in London to enjoy special exhibitions together; and even stayed in our home – Mary is no more.

Her ashes have joined those of her husband on the mountain where he met his death. We so miss her wonderful friendship.

Ambling to the Arctic Circle

That spring, when we arrived at the shed to fetch Bondo to again take up our life with her, we found, on trying to start her engine, that it was completely dead – so thinking the problem to be the battery we sent a message to the local garage and a new battery was brought and connected up. Still no life in the engine.

We then discovered that field mice had made their winter home in that part of the engine where there was a concentration of electric wiring. From this we learned that mice, like birds, build nests with tiny sticks and straw and that they enjoy a diet of rubber. After clearing the mess of the mice's winter nest the garage man made a temporary electrical connection, advising us to go to the auto-electric specialists in the town, some ten kilometres away, for a major re-wiring job.

This completed, we set out as planned on our long journey to the Arctic Circle. After completing about ten kilometres of that journey the engine suddenly burst into flame, spreading even to the dashboard. The auto-electricians had neglected to notice that the mice had chewed through the rubber piping which fed the petrol to the engine, so petrol had escaped on to the hot motor. Another major repair job also included a repeat of the rewiring just completed. The dashboard also had to be painted. This time we were entitled to make an insurance claim, so it was necessary to retrace our steps southwards; and abandon the Arctic Circle for much nearer Mont Blanc.

So the following year we once again set out for the north. We reached Basle on the first leg of our journey, not uneventful as we had to spend the weekend in Solothurn for repairs, as usual, but while waiting for the garage to open on Monday morning we enjoyed visiting this attractive town and also had a wonderful day walking in the forest nearby. However, en route to Basle we hit upon the idea that Bondo and ourselves should hitch a ride on a barge down the

Rhine to Rotterdam and from there board a ferry to Norway to save ourselves all that motoring.

On arrival in Basle we made straight for the Rhine harbour. As it was too late in the day to book our barge, we decided to spend the night very satisfactorily parked overlooking the ships, barges, cranes and dock-side warehouses. Next morning we walked across to the harbour offices; not only was it difficult to make ourselves understood in the language, but our request was so unusual that they had to find someone who spoke English to make sure that they really understood what we wanted. In perfect English we were told that barges have holds, not decks, so Bondo could not possibly be accommodated. Though he was too polite to say so, he implied that our request was quite ridiculous. Rather a pity – we had read and heard of the joys of cruises down the Rhine.

We returned to Bondo with no alternative but to continue our long drive north – but the engine would not start – the battery was dead! We set off on foot to find a garage. They came, tested our battery and recommended we purchase a new one. We were basically certain that it only needed recharging – but why had it run down? Considering the long journey ahead we agreed and with a brand new battery set out with our usual enthusiasm and optimism.

Skirting the Rhine, we decided to spend time in Strasbourg, that historic city reflecting its arched bridges and ancient towers in the river and network of canals – the view we had from where we 'stayed'. We visited the magnificent cathedral and many other points of interest in this lovely city.

On purchasing a more detailed map to study our route we discovered that there is a ferry service from Amsterdam to Bergen – so why should we travel the whole of this long distance by road? So, next stop Amsterdam! We did resist diverting to Metz to again see that magnificent Gothic cathedral and were also reminded of our visit to a trade fair there, the main attraction being a battery-powered car – what an excellent idea. From our recent experiences we know that an engine without a battery is useless, so who needs an engine!

That night we only got as far as Thionville where we slept on the large car park of the bus station, but next day we arrived in Luxembourg in time to join a conducted tour of the ancient ramparts and underground fortifications which we had not seen on our previous visit. Maybe they could accommodate the entire population of this

When we visit Basle we choose to 'live' on a riverside site on the mighty Rhine, deserted at night.

Here at the port of Basle we had hoped to board a barge with Bondo to sail down the river Rhine to Rotterdam.

mini-state, using them as shelters, and after the nuclear war Luxembourg would be the only surviving country in Europe!

That night we slept at Maastricht. After hunting around in the town we crossed a bridge and came upon a large car park by the river with trees among the parking bays, whose shade we did not need as it was raining when we woke next morning – how typical of weather in Holland.

To avoid the traffic on the main road we detoured on to a secondary road, crossed a bridge and stopped at a garage as Bondo's petrol gauge told us that it was time to fill up. We had a monetary problem – we offered the garage a Traveller's Cheque in our best Dutch, but they politely advised us to go to Holland, where a garage on the main road accepts Travellers' Cheques – we had inadvertently crossed into Belgium. Where better than Luxembourg to have done our banking business – but we were there on Saturday when banks are closed.

We recrossed the bridge and after a few miles reached the garage. Change from our Traveller's Cheque into gulden enabled us to buy food at the mini-market attached to the garage. We had lunch on the car park.

During the afternoon we arrived at Ijmuiden, from where our map indicated the ferry boat would leave for Bergen. There was no sign of any harbour, just a quiet village without a soul about on this Sunday afternoon. We found a police station and asked them to enquire for us when a ship would be leaving. Of course, being Sunday, there was no reply from the shipping office, so the police directed us up river to the Port of Amsterdam – mile upon mile of harbour basins, jetties, warehouses, transport vehicles etc. We got hopelessly lost and it was some time before we were finally directed to the harbour from which ferry boats left for Norway.

A boat was about to depart. There were no available cabins, they could only offer us seats. We intended doing just that, anyway. They sent a woman to measure Bondo. In her haste I think she erred or did us a favour with the extra twenty centimetres length which would have put Bondo in a higher price category. We drove aboard as the gangway was lifted behind us.

We did not know that all the upper deck seats were booked and ours were in the bowels of the ship. No one else was below decks with us. At that point we were far too interested in what was happening to the ship as she slowly cruised through a wide river-cum-canal towards giant sluice-gates. After some delay the sluice-gates opened and the ship passed through to the open sea. Our ship was now rolling on the ocean swells of the North Sea. We were tired from our long journey and had a good night.

By midday the sea was becoming very rough, Lynn went below to lie on her back as she usually does when seas are rough, but I, who had never been worried by rough seas, went to the self-service and imbibed an expensive meal. The boat began to roll and pitch mercilessly. I had difficulty descending the steep steps to reach our quarters below. Lynn was lying flat on her back, not that thrilled with life – having collected the blankets from several of the seats and made a bed on the floor. Apart from feeling a little queasy myself I started to worry about Bondo. Had they tied her down properly because we came on board so late? My mind started to run round in circles, I imagined Bondo rolling from one end of the hold to the other, as I now felt I was. Was I going to be seasick? I, who in all my long life of travel had prided myself that I had never succumbed and when everyone else on board was ill I had thoroughly enjoyed my meals in a deserted dining room. So this time I was! This was the North Sea, I told myself.

By late evening Lynn was groaning miserably. Our problem was that we were so low down in the boat. I crawled up the steep staircase on hands and knees and made my way to the purser's office to plead for a cabin. Impossible, none were vacant. Finally the purser took pity on me and said that only the sick-bay was vacant. "We are both certainly sick enough for that," I retorted. The rest of the night we spent comfortably tucked up in bed on an upper deck and slept off the effects.

How happy we were next morning to drive Bondo, none the worse for the pitch and roll, out of the hold on to the terra firma of our beloved Bergen.

Our choice of route this time, our second visit to Norway, was determined by a very warm invitation to join a very good Norwegian friend whom we had come to know in the years since our first visit. He is a surveyor with his government's Geographical Survey Department, and was at that time on field work in the Ostra district on the fjord route.

After a few enjoyable days in Bergen we set out. On reaching Knarvik, after crossing our first ferry, Lynn discovered that her set of car keys was missing. I had been driving. She was sure that she had left them at the garage on the edge of the city where we had filled up with our first Norwegian petrol. It was decided that instead of recrossing on the ferry and driving all the way back, Lynn would hitch a lift back to look for her keys. As a result she had two very pleasant encounters – one way with the headmaster of a high school, thus enabling her to ask questions about Norway's excellent educational system. She found her keys. Hitching her second lift back with an organiser of rock bands she learnt from him about military service in Norway.

In the meantime I waited under the large new bridge linking the mainland to one of the larger islands and got into conversation with a Malaysian family, Ma and Pa and six kids, who had parked for a break. They told me excitedly that they were on a thirty-day round the world tour, their final destination Mecca. They seemed a little vague as to where they had come from and how they would finally reach their objective. They were rather far from Mecca at this point and certainly far from home. I wondered if they would make it. The younger children were whimpering and restless. I guess they were less enthusiastic! Strange travellers one meets!

We spent our night below the bridge and continued on our way next morning. The road passed across a tongue of land between two fjords and then driving inland we passed tiny lakes with water lilies and edged with reeds. We were tempted to stop at each lake, they were so beautiful. In the late afternoon we stopped for tea and it started to rain. When we were ready to drive off, Bondo would not start – surely our new battery could not have run down, it must be self-starter trouble this time! We decided to walk back to the shop in the village we had passed a couple of miles back and where we had also shopped, to ask them to let me phone the nearest garage. The rain was pouring down steadily, so off I went under my umbrella and in my rain boots, arriving at the shop just as they were closing. The kindly lady said the garage was in the next village and phoned for me.

By the time I returned to Bondo the garage people had arrived in a jeep with tow ropes, etc. We did not exactly relish the idea of being towed along the narrow, winding road, quite heavily trafficked. We assured them that all we needed was a push to get the engine started.

Lindäs, 'Heaven on earth' – opposite a small rocky island, a 'holme' in Norwegian – with small birch trees growing on top – and beyond, across the water, a backdrop of range upon range of mountains.

Parked on a small jetty on the Fonnesbotjoen Fjord outside the village of Lindäs.

And so we reached the garage a few miles beyond on our own steam. By this time it was too late to do anything so we parked behind the garage which adjoined open country and settled down for the night. Instead of counting sheep to get to sleep I tried to count the number of times and in how many different countries we had slept behind garages. I fell asleep long before I had reached a final count.

Next morning the mechanic removed our self-starter and suggested replacing it with a second-hand spare he had, which he demonstrated to me – it sparked. I asked if he had given ours the same test. No... and proceeded to do so... The spark was very much stronger. Had he tested the battery? No... it was absolutely flat! He reinstalled our self-starter, changed our battery with the garage spare and Hey Presto! the engine sprang to life. The mechanic looked a little shame-faced. Did I hear Bondo chuckle? We were not impressed by his efficiency. Later when we paid the account he would not charge for the time spent on the self-starter. Perhaps it was partly our fault as we said we had a brand new battery. But why had it run down? Had Basle sold us a dud? He suggested we use his battery while he puts ours on a twenty-four-hour charge.

He gave us instructions on how to reach the fjord. We followed the road through the small village of Lindäs and after about three kilometres came to a Heaven on Earth – a small jetty on the edge of the fjord between two bays – how beautiful and how peaceful. Opposite was a small rocky island, a *holme* in Norwegian – with small birch trees growing on its top – and beyond across the water a backdrop of range upon range of mountains. We were looking towards the great Jostedalsbreen Glacier. The sky was overcast, heavy grey clouds moved about, changing the light continuously– now obscuring the sun and then a beam of light through a breach in the clouds, illuminating the little island – then a spot on the shore, and then on the distant range – for a split second the glistening white of snow on the faraway mountains.

The waters of the fjord were very still. A few small colourful boats moored in the little bays were mirror-reflected in the water. A few boats, bottoms up, lay on the grass. Up the fjord a small sea-plane landed and floated to the shore. After a short stop it floated away again disappearing out of sight among the islands.

A very small, blond, blue-eyed boy (he could not have been more than five years old) sat at the end of the pier, his tiny legs dangling over the edge, holding a stick over the water with a piece of string attached. He smiled up at us, he knew that we knew he would not catch a fish, but it was fun pretending. Other children were playing at the edge of the water, always with a ready smile. We loved this spontaneous friendliness which we found so endearing a characteristic of the Norwegian people. A man on a small tractor coming down the hill over a dusty track waved as he passed. We were having a lovely day. Who worries about batteries? We went walking to explore the rocky coves along the fjord and into the flower-filled fields.

When we returned 'home', an old man came to talk to us. "Never", he said in broken English, "will we Norwegians forget how the English helped us during the War." We invited him in for coffee. He said he had known English long ago, but had forgotten it. He had been to sea (what Norwegian has not) and visited Britain many times. A pity the conversation was limited. He offered to lend us his boat and fishing tackle for the next day – and indicated with outstretched arms that we would catch a fish that size. We were less optimistic about our fishing prowess, but excited at the prospect of boating on the fjord. We would land on an island like Robinson Crusoe.

Later in the evening two young boys in a boat held up a large fish, one of which they had caught, then came ashore to give us one. We naturally thought they were selling them. Oh no – a present! Lynn, of course, chose the smallest fish. Food-wise I am much greedier – we could have cooked for more than one day – on the other hand we may catch our own tomorrow! What an excellent supper we had that evening.

How disappointed we were when we woke next morning under a heavy canopy of dark cloud and pouring rain. It rained off and on most of the day. There seemed little point in waiting as tomorrow may be no different from today. We did not see the old man again, nor did we know where he lived. We would have liked to thank him for his kind offer.

We returned to the garage to collect our own battery, no wiser as to the reason why it had run down – only proof that we had not needed to purchase a new one in Basle. The battery mysteriously 'died' again and again during this trip.

We drove on for some miles to Leirvag and waited for the ferry to cross the Fensfjord to Slovag. It was still drizzling, the mist partly obscuring and mystifying the puzzling confusion of sea, fjords, islands and indented coast on one of the most broken coastlines to be found anywhere.

The drive from the ferry station was along a wild, barren rocky uninhabited coast and then through a narrow opening to a long narrow finger of a fjord in a gorgeous green fertile valley. The fjord was edged with reeds and short, pale green water grass. We parked for a late lunch at the waters' edge overlooking a small island topped with fir trees and with views on both sides of very steep forested mountain sides. There were many coloured wooden farmhouses set in emerald fields.

The rain had at last ceased. The sun came out and bathed the entire scene in that very special after-rain light on wet vegetation. It was so beautiful that we were rather reluctant to move on. At the end of the fjord a steep incline wound upwards in a series of hairpin bends to the top of the pass. From 2,200 feet we looked down on the Sognefjord, Norway's widest and longest fjord. Unfortunately the heavy dark clouds hid the tops of the mountains and the great glacier, Europe's largest, which we could have seen so well from this height. Far down below a ship like a tiny toy moved almost imperceptibly along the still waters of the Fjord.

As we came down the pass we passed the Brekkestranda Hotel on the edge of the fjord, of wood construction with grass growing on the roofs – another of Norway's traditional hotels which was patronised in the last century when only aristocracy could afford to travel.

We had reached Brekke, seventy kilometres from Bergen and five days later!

*

We spent that night in the little town of Brekke on the car park outside the Bank (it was Saturday night) – better on the tarmac as the ground was very wet.

The next morning we walked across a bridge over the river, up the valley which stretched back from the fjord towards the mountains to see the farms with their pastel-shaded wooden houses and reddish-brown farm buildings.

We had missed the midday ferry which we had intended to take and left at 2 p.m. for our longest crossing over the Sognefjord. We were so disappointed that it rained most of the way, but when we landed at Lavik the sun came out, so we had the full benefit of the drive which skirted the edge of the fjord, at first almost level with the water, passing tiny inlets with grey rock ledges and small islands or 'holmes'. The road then rose well above the fjord giving us spectacular views up the fjord to the snow-covered mountains of the Stols-heimen. There were magnificent cloud effects across the water. Pale green valleys and tiny dots of houses were backed by deep dark clefts in the ice-speckled mountains rising above and with heavy clouds swirling around them.

The road rounded a peninsula which formed one side of the opening to an arm of the fjord and turned at right angles to follow it, in the direction of the mountains, between huge boulders.

The views to the end of the arm of the fjord were breathtaking, a deep cut between the mountains and range upon range beyond. A rounded cone-shaped mountain dwarfed the little town of Vadheim. As we drove into Vadheim we passed some modern wooden houses, each a different colour – light green, dark green, tan, brown, terracotta and dark red. The town has an electro-industry.

We stopped for supper near the pier and watched the comings and goings of the town's folk. How they must love their beautiful little town. It was too public and too early for a night stop, so we decided to push on. We never had to worry about night drawing in – it never did.

Leaving the town we passed through the narrow gap, the road following a fast-flowing river. On its banks was a beautiful phenomenon – the rocks of the scree up the slope were covered with smooth, green, velvet-like moss. We followed the rushing river to its exit from a dark, silent *vatn* (lake). Unfortunately it was dull and raining again, otherwise we would have been tempted to walk in this lovely area. On each side of the narrow valley the mountains towered above us with waterfalls cascading down.

We reached the small modern town of Steinen with a beautiful modern school on a rise above the town. We drove on to find somewhere to sleep in this lovely valley. Ahead was a swollen river with reeds and grass on its bank half-submerged under water. There was nowhere to stop. The road now rose steeply through a narrow, heavily forested pass. From the top wonderful views of the mountains around and we were looking down on the town of Forde at the head of its fjord.

In the town we found ideal parking at the edge of a small inlet from the river, a spur of grass bank with trees growing on it, cutting it off from the main fast-flowing river which entered the fjord beyond. Small, colourful boats lay anchored in the water below us. Coloured wooden houses set among trees and gardens crept up the slopes to the forested mountain above. We settled down happily for the night.

Next day it was raining, heavily at times, a good excuse for a lazy day. Between showers we visited the town and did our shopping at Domus, Norway's largest departmental chain, which had a beautiful shop in this town.

Shortly after leaving Forde we came upon an agricultural school. Of course, we could not resist visiting it, so parked at the side of the road and chatted to students fixing fences, just one of the jobs I had done as a student on an agricultural training farm, in my youth. They told us that if we walked on we would come to a most beautiful waterfall – that, too, we could not resist. An enormous volume of water roared down through a gap in the mountainside and splashed into a river rushing past. There seems to be no limits to the extravaganza of nature in this country. We walked across the fields to the college farm buildings. There were rows of cages which we thought housed rabbits, but found that they contained small foxes, bred no doubt for their fur.

After a stop for breakfast we reached the long, narrow Jolstervatn, high mountains reflecting into the still waters of the lake. We travelled for about ten kilometres along it at horse and cart pace so as to enjoy the view to the full. How much one misses when travelling in a fast-moving vehicle.

At Byrkjelo we stopped for petrol, eastwards leading to Olden and Stryn where we eventually intended going, but first to Orsta to visit our friend, so turned westwards into a narrow valley, the turquoise-coloured water of a wide river coming off the glacier not far to the east of us, rushing down with tremendous speed and power, foaming over stones and spraying against boulder obstructions. Above us, yet another waterfall tumbled down from the mountain top, 1,500 feet above. At first one complete fall, then a wide fan of water over a smooth rock face and then in a series of cascades adding its waters to the already powerful flow of the river below. As the valley opened up there were several small farms with cows and fields of fodder and vegetable patches beside the homesteads. Whole families were haymaking, hanging the hay to dry on long, temporarily constructed fences. We wondered how they could make a living on such small areas. We were told later, when we asked, that the farmers also supplemented their income with forestry and fishing. There are no direct farm subsidies, but the Government assures good prices for farm products and reasonable prices to the consumer.

After doing our usual shopping for supplies in the modern town of Sandane we drove along the Gloppenfjord to the ferry harbour at Anda on the Nordfjord. Here we chatted to an ex-Glaswegian who, with his four children, was awaiting the next ferry. He told us that he had come to Norway on holiday, met a Norwegian girl and never gone back to Glasgow. He advised us to stay the night on this side of the fjord, as we would not find satisfactory parking at Lote on the opposite side.

So we took up very satisfactory residence in the woods at the edge of the ferry car park, with wonderful views across the fjord. Later, annoyingly, a large 'monster' (lorry and trailer), which had apparently missed the last ferry of the day, parked in front of us blocking our view, but when we awoke next morning he had already gone.

During the night I had a nightmare – that we entered the unlit tunnel and our lights failed. I woke in a cold sweat. It was a comfort that it is daylight all night, so nightmares are not too frightening.

However, we took a walk along the peninsula dividing the Nordfjord from the branch fjord we had come along the day before, to inspect the tiny lighthouse, then returned 'home' through the woods for a late breakfast. A passenger liner glided past scarcely disturbing the quiet waters of the fjord.

We crossed at midday – spectacular views up and down the fjord to the mountains, the coast we had left and to the unknown ahead. The crossing was only too short and we landed at Lote. Driving up a steep incline we stopped for some time to look down on the spectacular views on all sides, to watch the drama of changing light and colours caused by the movement of clouds and their shadows over the tranquil waters of the fjord, now far down below us, and the changing forms of the mountains beyond. We could only just discern the little lighthouse we had visited on the peninsula protruding forward and backed by the arm of the fjord which penetrated deep into the shadows between the mountains. A shower of rain in the far distance like a white curtain gradually obliterated part of the scene.

We entered the long tunnel – wide and well lit – so we did not need to try out our lights. We met no other vehicles and emerged into a gentle and less dramatic landscape of rolling hills and grassland.

The town of Nordfjordheid, one of the oldest in this area, has an old-world charm with its white, wooden, traditional style architecture. It is the centre of the famous and beloved Nordfjord horse, probably the oldest and most original horses in Europe. It is a sturdy small horse, light in colour with stiff upright mane and a dark streak along its back, features only found in the original wild horses. We had close acquaintance with these lovely creatures during our time spent in western Norway.

There were more valleys, mountains and forests, more waterfalls, rivers, lakes and fjords until our final crossing of the Voldafjord to Volda and until we finally reached Orsta. It was our fifth ferry crossing. We often wonder whether in western Norway the roads are extensions of the ferries or the ferries extensions of the roads.

We received a grand welcome when we arrived at the camp where our friend was staying in his tent while on survey fieldwork in the district. We had dinner together in Bondo and celebrated a happy reunion. Somewhat amused at the length of time it had taken us to travel from Bergen to Orsta, he suggested that we leave Bondo in the camp, as he would like to drive us by car to Trondheim, from where we could take train and buses to reach the far north. What a lovely day's trip we had and with what a knowledgeable guide.

We reached Narvik, well beyond the Arctic Circle. How we missed dear old Bondo when we arrived at the bus terminal and dragged our little suitcases through the pouring rain in search of an hotel and how claustrophobic to be confined in an hotel bedroom. By the next morning the weather had so deteriorated that the clouds were at street level.

Not only did we not see the midnight sun, we did not even see the midday sun! The tourist office held out no hope for better conditions in the days ahead – so we never reached Noordkapp – we only had another 612 kilometres to go! Bondo never reached the Arctic Circle, but at least we did.

We had travelled by car, train and bus 2,738 kilometres. How long would that distance have taken us with Bondo!

*

'Flu on the Fjord

When we returned from our northern adventure it was necessary to take Bondo out of the camp at Orsta, as the weather was as bad as it was up north and the camp was a bog. Bondo needed to stand on tarmac.

Our friend recommended a visit to one of the islands famous for its bird life, so in preparation for this trip we drove to the ferry station at Rejanes a few miles beyond Orsta, where we were able to park in a half-hidden corner round a bend on the very edge of the fjord.

I had arrived back from the Arctic Circle with a heavy cold, which developed into a bad dose of 'flu. 'Flu, of course, is no fun anywhere, but if one has to suffer it, where better than in Bondo on a fjord?

It rained steadily pit-a-pat on Bondo's roof and streamed in rivulets down the windows. I was so cosy tucked up in my sleeping bag and under blankets, Lynn administering, at arm's length, aspirins and hot drinks at all hours of the day and night. Through the windows, without lifting my head, I could look out across the fjord and up to the strange-shaped mountain above us, the scene disappearing and reappearing as the rain eased off and the mist lifted for a while.

It was no darker at night than during the day, so that time lost all meaning. My fever gave it all a dreamlike quality. I felt completely lethargic and utterly content. Days passed. The ferryboat crew must have wondered when we would come aboard! Our friend visited every evening with gifts of chocolates. When the weather worsened and the mountain was powdered with fresh snow he suggested we take a room or move into an hotel. I refused to be closeted in a room, and where else would Lynn be able to administer to me so conveniently with our little kitchen at hand, and when she had to go shopping it was only a short drive up the hill to a little shop, but too far to walk in the rain, so I remained in bed in Bondo and enjoyed a change of scene.

So having 'flu on the fjord was not so bad. When the fever was over and the weather improved, although not fit for the planned excursion to the bird island, we continued on our way coughing and convalescing at 'home'.

The Garage Trail through Europe

Though we love her dearly we have to admit that Bondo has some extremely exasperating characteristics - she is a terrible tease and has a somewhat sadistic sense of humour. We have, of course, to make allowances for her age, she has been with us now for so many years and was four years old when she came to us. In some ways she is healthier now than when we first met her.

Admittedly she has had a considerable number of transplants in the course of time - carburettor, transmissions, brake cylinders, brake linings, wheel and steering bearings, exhaust, clutch plate, water pump, radiator repair, new tyres, a few batteries; complete renewal of electric wiring and rubber piping which had been eaten by field mice who use Bondo as their 'home' during the cold Swiss winters. We have even had to replace a window broken by vandals at Aigues Mortes in the south of France.

Each and every one of these operations are just part of the adventure of living with Bondo. When anything goes wrong it invariably happens on a Friday, so that nothing can be done until Monday. We have lost count of how many times we have slept behind a garage.

On one occasion she decided to stall right on the border with her front wheels in Switzerland and her back wheels in France - there she stood and refused to budge - so embarrassing for us when the furious customs police had to push us aside to release a mile of traffic piled up behind us.

When the engine went up in flames in Avenches as we were passing through the town, our first ten miles en route to the Arctic Circle, and having doused the flames with water from our small domestic containers, we found that we had drawn up exactly under a garage sign - G.M. Bedford (the make of our caravan). After closing time, of course. Was that Bondo's idea of asking forgiveness? It was not her fault that time – that is part of the mice story. With some help from passers-by we pushed her behind the garage and there we spent the night. Next day Bondo again underwent complete rewiring within twenty-four hours of being rewired after mice nesting.

But we must give Bondo credit for one thing. She has never really let us down, we have always been able to limp to a garage so we have never had to be towed. Only twice, in all these years, have we had to leave 'home' to sleep in an hotel. Thanks to Swiss efficiency, engine reconditioning was completed within one week – that occasion we spent in Denise's lake-side mobile home.

These breakdowns more often than not result in our discovering beautiful and interesting places to visit and forging new friendships, whereas ordinarily one may just drive through en route to a planned destination. We also gain insight into the characters, whether kindly or otherwise, of garage personnel.

At the very beginning of our travels with Bondo, while en route to Patras on the Isthmus of Corinth to board a ferryboat across the Adriatic to Italy, the engine suddenly petered out. By some stroke of luck she did start up again and we reached Patras. En route to the harbour she again petered out in a scruffy street in front of some sort of metal workshop. People in the street noticing our dilemma called the man from the workshop to see if he could help us. He indicated that our problem might be 'eletreek' and went off down the street, returning with his friend, an auto-electrician, who started tinkering with the wiring and testing here and there. We wondered whether he knew what he was doing! We were in rather a panic as we were due to board our ship within the hour.

Meanwhile the man from the workshop crept underneath Bondo and indicated that we had a hole in the exhaust the size of his fist. He disappeared into his workshop, emerged with a tool to detach the damaged section of the exhaust and took it back into the workshop. It was some time before he emerged with his blowpipe and a piece of pipe which he had fashioned to fit, which he duly welded to the existing pipe.

At the same time the electrician had found and repaired the fault and with a whoop of triumph he started the engine.

It was already 8.30 p.m. when the jobs were completed and our saviours presented their account – a quarter of what the jobs would cost according to our reckoning. They could have charged us the earth under the circumstances! Where else in the world could one expect work to continue so long after hours? This endeared us to the Greek people.

We only just made it to the ship, but only because sailing was delayed.

On arrival at Ancona in Italy we spent several days on the coast as the weather was very hot, but in an effort to go up to the Apennines and Assisi, Bondo boiled so that we had to turn back to Mascerata. This was Friday evening and a garage there told us that our radiator required cleaning, but they could not start the job before Monday. Stupidly, we did not wait over the weekend, as we had already spent a few days in this interesting town and could not go back to our excellent camp in the Giardini because of the peeping toms, so we decided to push on.

Bondo's habit of running a temperature at the least provocation dogged us for a long time and certainly was the cause of many subsequent problems, even to the need of new valves, which became burnt out, and new carburettor, for which we waited a week in Biarritz as it had to be ordered from Paris or England – to this day we are not sure where it came from.

In complete contrast to our Patras experience, when reaching Switzerland and after having spent many weeks there, we were finally able to solve the problem of our leaking roof, caused by an overhanging branch of a tree in our desperate bid to find shade below the Acropolis in the summer heat of Greece. Bondo's body is made of fibreglass.

We had been directed to a boat-building workshop at Spiez on Lake Thun that specialised in fibre-glass repairs. We were shown into an office and entered into the appointment book for a time the next day, like making an appointment for the doctor or dentist. It would cost us thirty Swiss francs per hour, we were told. The following day, at the appointed hour, we drove our Bondo into the 'operating theatre', a hygienic and very orderly shed with white-coated 'doctors' in attendance. We were not allowed to witness the 'plastic surgery operation' and told to return in the late afternoon. However, we returned one and a half hours later to see how the patient was progressing. She was ready, the charge now Sw. Frs. 82. We protested. No explanation was offered – "if the price does not suit you you can leave your vehicle here." Irritated and annoyed we paid up, remembering with nostalgia the kindness and consideration and under-charging in the dirty back street in Patras.

While on the subject of fibre-glass repairs we are reminded of our other experiences which have involved us with boat builders on Swiss lakes over the years.

On one occasion Do backed into a pole which she did not expect to be there, in the middle of a driveway, as divider between right and left, and seriously bashed in the back door of Bondo. We were directed here and there to possible repairers. One firm suggested an aluminium patch, but we could not, under any circumstances, allow Bondo to go through life with such a disfiguring scar. So we drove off to Yverdon to investigate whether we could find a saner solution somewhere near where we often parked outside the Yachting Club House. We found a small workshop just a couple of hundred yards up the road, run by a very charming young man with a passion for boats. He spoke perfect English, always a great help as our French is never good enough to negotiate the technical problems we so often encounter. Of course he could do the job, but he would have to remove the door and it would take a couple of days, which presented a problem – but we had no alternative.

So he removed the door and we drove off to our parking place between boats parked on the shore, which were kept there either for repairs or as storage at the end of the summer season.

We hung our spare blanket across the doorway to keep out draughts, albeit not very adequately. During the night we were awakened by thunder and lightning warning of a pending storm. We hastily unpacked a sheet of black plastic and improvised a curtain, securing it over the blanket with clothes pegs. Just in time. The rain came down in torrents.

*

We had been living, as usual, in one of our favourite and most convenient spots – the parking lot for the yachting harbour at Estavayer-le-Lac. On this occasion, before leaving for somewhere else, it was necessary to park in the town to do some shopping and go to the post office (usually we walk to the town for food shopping). We found convenient parking at the top of the road.

Estavayer-le-Lac is a medieval walled town (circa twelfth century) on a hill which has not been able to come to terms with the horrific traffic problems of the twentieth century.

On a pole at the top of that road there hangs a large triangular sign with an arrow pointing *toutes directions*. Having completed our business we prepared to drive off. Just at that moment an enormous lorry was coming up the road so Lynn drove forward to allow it to pass before turning into the road. There was a frightening crash – we thought the lorry had bashed into us. I jumped out of Bondo to find that Lynn had driven *toutes directions*, crashing into the sign and embedding the point of the sign in our roof. The top window was smashed, from the inside of Bondo we could see nothing until we opened the small cupboard above the sink and there was the point of the sign at least ten centimetres inside with crushed fibreglass around it. We could move neither forward nor backwards. I went off in search of the police – usually not much in evidence in Swiss towns.

Eventually two policemen arrived. The only way to release us would be to remove the sign from the roof. They sent for a ladder and tools. They unscrewed the bolts holding the sign to its pole, forcibly pushed it up from Bondo's roof and rescrewing it high enough to allow us to drive out from under it. To this day that sign remains just that much higher.

We U-turned down the road to the large boat sales and repair business near the lake. No, they were much too busy to take on another job, opined the unkindly manageress. By chance an artisan, who spoke English, appeared. We begged him to help us. After all the job was an emergency and we would be in terrible trouble if it rained. He agreed to do an emergency job by sealing the roof, but would not be able to give it a finish. But at least there would not be a leak. To this day they have never found time to do the finishing job and so Bondo bears a large dark head scar, just like Mikael Gorbachev.

The next day we drove to the caravan supply shop to have a new top window fitted, which in the meantime had been covered by a plastic bag.

*

Before leaving Edinburgh for Norway that second summer of Life with Bondo we were taken by a friend to a recommended General

Motors Garage to which category Bondo belonged, and gave them instructions to make a thorough inspection and to undertake any necessary repairs as we were two women travelling alone and intended covering many miles through Scandinavia and finally on to the south of Europe.

Some twenty miles out of Edinburgh, en route to Newcastle to take ship to Bergen, the engine started making a strange puffing sound and losing power. On opening the engine we discovered that the garage had forgotten to replace the oil-cap after changing the oil, so we covered it with a piece of plastic in a Heath Robinson manner. We telephoned them and they had the impudence to tell us to go to G.M. garage in Newcastle. We refused to go hunting their branch in Newcastle, a city which we did not know and instructed them to send the cap to Bergen. In the event the parcel caught up with us in Voss two and a half weeks later containing not an oil cap but an oil filter!

Soon after leaving Bergen we felt that there was something wrong with the steering. We reached a village where we saw a man working underneath his car and asked him if he would check our steering. He could find no fault. So we carried on. Some days later we noticed that one of the tyres was wearing unevenly, and had them changed around.

Thereafter we had to rather limit our travels around the fjords because of bad tyres. We had so wanted to drive up to the Jostedalsbreen Glacier, the largest on the continent of Europe, 483 square miles, on a rough road of twenty-three miles, to view tributaries of this glacier. This was a great disappointment.

We decided that we must do something about obtaining new tyres when we would finally reach Oslo, as we could not obtain our outlandish size among the fjord towns.

However, after many more miles and weeks, part of the way on gravel roads, we reached Oslo and made our way to the Goodyear Tyre agents, after seeing a huge advertising sign in the sky. There we met Mr Andersen, a most charming man who spoke perfect English, having spent some time in the United States. He took us to their tyre vulcanising department to have our tyres examined and they found that one tyre was a completely different size from the other three. Why did not Edinburgh discover this fault? Mr Andersen was horrified and told us that we were very silly girls to travel with such tyres! No wonder we thought there was something wrong with the steering!

He did not have our size in stock, but told us to return at 1 p.m. by which time he would have phoned around Norway, Sweden and Denmark in an attempt to locate the correct size tyres.

We spent the morning wandering around a rather dreary part of Oslo. We were not very impressed with our first day, but subsequently found the attractive and interesting parts of Oslo and spent several more days there. However on return to Mr Andersen he informed us that no 070 size tyres were available in Scandinavia and the vulcaniser offered us one German tyre at an exorbitant price; but one tyre was of no use as we required two, so we decided against that, apart from the fact that we avoid buying German goods.

That night we spent outside the St Hanshaugen Park, a rather disturbed night at that because cars came screeching their tyres up the hill. How the Norwegians wear out their tyres, something we were very much aware of in view of our current preoccupation with tyres.

During the weekend we discovered the Frognor Park with the Vigeland Sculptures and a perfect site to camp. On Monday morning as we drove out of the Park we suddenly came upon a Fiat agency and thought that perhaps we would be able to obtain Pirelli tyres from them. The manager was more than helpful. He spent a whole hour telephoning around to locate our size tyres and even though everyone at the other end of the phone said no hope, he would not give up trying. Finally his persistence was rewarded and he again gave us his time, giving us detailed instructions on how to find Dekk & Pigg on the other side of the city. We duly arrived and found them waiting in the street for us. Immediately they fitted two Danish retreads at a reasonable price. These tyres proved to be as good as new ones of the very best make. The manager then took us to his bank to change travellers cheques to pay for the tyres. He then guided us to the Akerhus Slott where we nearly passed out as the temperature was thirty-five degrees.

A few days later, while we were still camped in the Frognor Park, enjoying our stay there, we went back to Dekk & Pigg as we thought it would be a good idea to buy a spare tyre from them, but Mr Pigg would not sell us one as he said it would only deteriorate underneath the vehicle where the spare is housed. How honest of him, he could so easily have made another sale!

*

Moirans

While we were visiting Bern and driving down the main street of that city, we were suddenly aware of a clanking sound and wondered whether we were losing a wheel or something. We drew up into the first available parking space. I took out one of our mats and lay beneath Bondo to see whether anything was loose – a little undignified, I admit, when I realised we were just outside those prestigious buildings of the Swiss Federal Parliament. I could find nothing, but none the less we decided to go back to the area where our friend lived and discuss with him the possible cause and the best garage to go to. On the forty kilometre drive we heard that sound only once and when we drove with our friend and eventually the garage mechanic, Bondo was annoyingly silent. So the garage did some other repair which could have had no possible connection with the problem. I thought it was the universal joint, having had previous experience with a car I owned. The brakes were also tested at our request!

So we set off on our planned trip to France and Spain. Climbing a pass not far from Geneva and of no particular gradient we could not understand why Bondo was finding it so difficult and boiling like a kettle. We stopped to examine her. One wheelcap was so hot that I could not touch it. Had I been driving with the brakes on? I knew that I had not. We cooled down and eventually reached Annecy. We found the G.M. garage, where it was discovered that the last garage, on supposedly testing the brakes, had tightened them. This garage also advised us to have the radiator cleaned. It was, as usual, Friday afternoon, so we would have to return on Monday.

We drove on along the lake and found a tiny camp at Menthon St Bernard. On the mountain above us was the castle where the famous St Bernard was born. When clouds passed below the mountain the castle above looked like a fairy castle floating in the sky. We climbed the mountain to visit the castle.

While the radiator was sent to be cleaned we visited Annecy, that lovely French town on the edge of the lake with its two rivers flowing through the old town and the lovely bridges that crossed them. This was Rousseau's favourite town where he spent much time and did some of his writing.

Incidentally, the cleaning of the radiator did not cure Bondo's temperature!

The following Friday afternoon as we approached the small town of Moirans (some twenty miles from Grenoble), the Bern clank exhibited itself again, this time with a vengeance.

So once again we went to seek out a garage. Very soon there appeared arrows pointing to a garage centre. Winding noisily through the narrow street of this very old town we reached the garage on La Place de la Vieille Église – an eleventh-century church, now derelict.

Edouard Peretti, the garage owner, immediately drove Bondo around the village. It was the front universal joint, he thought, which he confirmed when crawling underneath to check. I had been right in my own diagnosis, but no one had believed me. Mr Peretti phoned a spares supplier in Grenoble, but they did not seem to have the part for our Bedford; even the chassis number did not help them to identify it. By then it was 5 p.m. and he would have to phone to Paris, but not until Monday morning, and then it may take a week to arrive.

The secretary in the garage office phoned the Mayor to obtain permission for us to park on the small sports field, entered through a gate, adjoining the old church on the opposite side of the garage. The area had no doubt been the ancient cemetery. What luck! We parked ourselves under two enormous ancient plane trees, very private. Just outside the gates there were facilities of a sort. We were in France! The sounds of 'Auld Lang Syne' being played by a brass band emanated from the back of the old church, probably the old vestry, now used as a club room.

A sweet young girl and her good-looking boyfriend were sent by the garage because they knew English as inadequately as Lynn knew French. They showed us where there was a water tap in the next lane for our convenience.

After a short rest we went to investigate our environs and saw a notice about a concert – piano and violin recital – that evening at the Salle de Fête in aid of the restoration of the old church. We decided to go as we would have many evenings with nothing to do. Jacques Durand-Bricaud, violinist, and Christian Bern, pianist, gave most enjoyable renderings of Mozart, Beethoven, Paulenc and Debussy.

After the concert a nice young man who knew English spoke to us. He said that he was personally interested in the restoration of the church as his family, going back many generations, had owned the stately home in the village, now also in a bad state because it had been used by the German army during World War Two. The church was a fine example of Romanesque with a finely pointed stone tower. The young girl with him suggested that we take a coach to Voirons to visit wine cellars and castles.

We had a wonderful quiet night and were awakened at eight o'clock by two clocks striking before and after the hour. After coffee we went to town to buy bread for our breakfast, and at the same time to the post office to arrange for our mail to be redirected to Moirans. The Hôtel de Ville was a beautiful seventeenth-century building, but the post office was very modern, all within a stone's throw of our 'home' – very convenient. Later we went back to the market on City Hall square, just in time before they packed up, and bought excellent cheeses, fresh milk, fresh farm eggs and cherries.

During the afternoon children came to play football and were all very intrigued by us. Our conversation with them was unfortunately rather difficult because of the language barrier. One little fellow informed us that his sister was a *professeur* of English and volunteered to bring her to visit us. She was a charming girl of about twenty. She and her little brother came in for coffee. Their father was the Postmaster. She spoke excellent English; after her studies in English she had spent some time in England as an au pair. She was married, lived in Grenoble and worked at the University. She invited us for the following Friday, her day off, to come to Grenoble and she would show us the town – which we did and could not have had a more knowledgeable guide to that interesting city.

In the early evening the little boy, accompanied by small friend, returned with an enormous bag of cherries. Later, his small friend, not to be outdone, brought more cherries. We had never before seen so many cherries together – we ate ourselves silly. We were touched by such kindness. At the same time a brass band, followed by choir practice in the old church, regaled our ears.

The next morning, Sunday, I was having my bath when there was a knock at the door. Lynn quickly put on some clothes and went out. It was the Postmaster who came to invite us to a special service in the church. He said we must come to hear the choir. We hurried to get ready to attend the service. It was very simple, more Protestant than Catholic, we thought. We were later to learn of the new reforms in the church in France. It was a lay choir of small girls and men and women accompanied by an excellent organist. It was very beautiful. At the end of the service the congregation received communion. When it was over the Postmaster came over to shake hands and we went out onto the church square where they were holding a bazaar. There were stalls selling cakes and baby clothes and other knickknacks as well as hot dogs. We bought some cakes and were just about to buy hot dogs for our lunch when the postmaster came over to us bringing an extremely good-looking youngish couple, whom we had noticed in the church. They spoke English, though not very fluently. He invited us to a glass of champagne which was being sold at one of the stalls. They invited us to join them in a restaurant for lunch. They would call for us, where we were parked, in an hour. We were quite taken aback by all the kindness and their hospitality. We were feeling pretty good from the champagne on our empty stomachs, not having had time for breakfast.

They took us to a very exclusive grill restaurant at the edge of the town – lunch was served on the terrace on this glorious summer's day, with lovely views to the mountains. We had 'bloody' beef on the rib, roast potato pebbles and salad and wine served from a jug. The dessert was the speciality of the area – a kind of white cheese and cream served with sugar. The cooking and service was with the elegance only the French possess.

Barbara came from the Black Forest country in Germany. She was dark and petite with upturned nose and a quiet gentle manner. Jean-Louis was from this area and owned a family concern manufacturing commercial stationery. Their fathers had been old business associates and so they had met.

After lunch they took us to their home. And what a home. Modern, with deep overhanging eaves half covering the outdoor terrace, heavy wooden-framed doors and windows, beautiful wood floors, wood panelled walls and beamed ceilings. Everything of the best in excellent taste. The house which Barbara showed us was most practically designed and with a suite downstairs, no doubt for visiting parents and friends. The basement included a large playroom for the children and a workshop for Barbara, whose hobby was woodwork. Her husband had given her a woodworking machine for her thirtieth birthday.

We sat out on the terrace. The house stood on a slight rise with extensive lawns sweeping down the slope, broken by flowerbeds and fruit trees, commanding magnificent views to the open country and to the Chartreuse mountains rising in the distance with grey cliff faces.

Jean-Louis excused himself as he had work to do. Barbara told us that she found much in France that was very different. She complained of a lack of creative encouragement in the kindergarten. She felt that children were taught too seriously at too young an age; that the school day was too long and did not allow sufficient time for independent play. She said that generally the French worked too hard, were too serious and lacked a sense of humour. We were somewhat taken aback. Were these not German characteristics and exactly what the French-speaking Swiss think of the German-speaking Swiss – "The French work to live, while the Germans live to work."

They brought us 'home' in the late afternoon. Jean-Louis offered us any help we might need, such as telexing Paris from his business, if necessary. Barbara invited us to come and sit in their garden any time we wished. Again we were overwhelmed by their kindness and thoughtfulness to complete strangers.

At about ten o'clock on Monday morning Mr Peretti came to us, telling us that he had again spoken to Grenoble who suggested that he bring the damaged part as a sample and perhaps they could match it. Soon after, the mechanic arrived with a large jack, lifted Bondo and removed the part. How convenient – not even disturbing us at 'home'.

While we were having our afternoon tea, a charming, sweet-faced, rather plump lady arrived. She introduced herself as the neighbour of Jean-Louis and Barbara. She said she would fetch us on Wednesday at midday and would drive us to Chartreuse to visit that famous monastery. Our social life in Moirans was becoming progressively more interesting!

The afternoon was somewhat restless, the children playing around us and at regular intervals coming to talk to us. Later we went for a walk through this rather scruffy part of the town but further on came to larger houses with gardens with beautiful rose bushes and the most enormous rose tree that we had ever seen. It seems that roses do particularly well in these parts. A swimming pool, now closed, held out other attractions for life in Moirans.

As we returned 'home' a small girl waylaid us to tell us that a lady in a white car had been looking for us. Obviously Barbara.

The next morning, while we were still in bed, we felt the car rising up under us. The mechanic had come to fit the new universal joint. Apparently Mr Peretti had managed to obtain it in Grenoble the previous afternoon. Bondo was now all set to go, but we were not.

There was tomorrow's date for Chartreuse and Friday's date for the visit to Grenoble; and in any case we also had to wait for our mail which was being redirected. Barbara arrived during the morning and went with us to the bank to change travellers' cheques to pay the garage. The price was more than reasonable. Mr Peretti had been efficient and in every way helpful.

Barbara again invited us to her home that afternoon. We could now come under our own steam, parking Bondo in her driveway. She insisted on our giving her our laundry which she arranged with her maid to put into the washing machine, and suggested that we take hot showers, which we did with great enjoyment. She also insisted that we stay for supper. Jean-Louis had gone to Paris on business and she was alone with the children. We had the meal on the terrace watching the distant mountains fading as the sun set.

Next day Mrs Gilot arrived as arranged. She took us home for lunch. What a contrast to their neighbours next door. An old house set among large trees in an unkempt garden. We went through an untidy hall and upstairs to the dining room, where the professor greeted us shyly struggling with his English. We were introduced to the children, Sylvie (fourteen), François (thirteen) and Jean-Pierre (ten), dark with curly hair and flat African nose, obviously adopted (from Martinique we learned from Barbara), as also were the other two French children. What wonderful people to adopt three children, from problem homes no doubt, and give them a loving home.

We spoke about the University of Grenoble where the professor taught French literature, specialising in eighteenth-century literature, the period of Voltaire and Rousseau. He spoke of the unrest among students in French universities, now even worse than the revolution of 1968. It was not clear what the students really wanted but only what they did not want. The professor tried to encourage the elder children to speak English to us which they were learning at school, but they ignored us. But little Jean-Pierre was friendly and full of smiles. He kept passing things round.

We asked about the war period in these parts. Mrs Gilot said her father had been with the Resistance and told us some stories of his and his companions dangerous adventures with the Gestapo. One rather strange story – a farmer was hiding three resistance fighters in his home when the Gestapo came to look for them. They escaped through a window. When the owner of the house was suspiciously asked to explain why there were three warm beds he replied that he had a high fever and was so hot that he moved from bed to bed for relief. The Gestapo demanded a thermometer. It was a miracle! He had a temperature, probably from fright. How difficult it is to understand how the Germans were able to take over this vast country. The more we travelled in France the more difficult it was to understand.

After lunch we went off with Mrs G. in her jalopy, an ancient Renault, to the famous monastery of Chartreuse. She drove at dangerous speed, rather spoiling for us the beautiful drive through thick forests towards the mountain. We passed through the village of St Laurent de Pont and crossed the bridge of St Bruno, named for the founder of the ancient Carthusian order of monks dating back to the twelfth century and who still occupy this famous monastery. The monks, avowed to silence and prayer, also work the farm and produce the well-known Chartreuse Liqueurs which we bought to give as presents to our friends. In their museum we learnt something of the life of the monks and were shown one of the cells in which they sleep, study and pray.

Three days later, after collecting our important mail at the post office, we said good-bye and thanks to the kind Postmaster and then went to bid farewell and thank the Mayor. He too did not know a word of English and spoke rapidly in French of which we did not understand a word, so Lynn responded in her best French. Then farewells to our new friends with whom we were to remain in contact all these years and have returned to visit. Sadly Jean-Louis died two years later leaving Barbara a young widow to bring up her three sons alone. The Gilots have had problems with their adopted children who did not want to study as the professor had so hoped.

We have Bondo's universal joint to thank for the most enjoyable week in Moirans in the Isère, making new friends whose kindness and hospitality we will always remember.

Bondo willing we will yet again visit them.

*

Epinal Episode

It was some years later that we were to have an experience in France which was in complete contrast to Moirans.

We were en route to Holland to meet South African cousins, from where we intended continuing on to Britain. We drove into Epinal, in the Vosges, in the late afternoon, took a stroll around this town attractively situated on the wide, fast-flowing River Moselle, a town which had been in the front line during two World Wars.

Beyond the beautiful town gardens was a large parking area. We settled down for the night under lovely trees overlooking the river.

Epinal is famous for having one of the earliest printing presses in Europe and pioneering colour printing. We visited the Imagerie Pellerin, a firm established during the seventeenth century that has an interesting working museum illustrating the historic development of printing processes. Today they specialise in colour prints of cartoons and illustrations of children's stories. We also visited the Museum which houses an interesting collection of old manuscripts and prints. The museum attendant in the print section told us that there was an expert restorer in Epinal who did work for the museum. We had with us an old print which had been in our family for many years and which we intended taking to Amsterdam and London for evaluation. It was in a rather poor state so we decided to take it to the restorer. He considered it well worth treating as it was a print of the work of a well known Dutch artist. We decided to delay our departure. His restoration was perfect. He had, in the meantime, referred to details about the artist. He was born in Holland at the end of the eighteenth century, later worked in Paris where our print was made and prices were listed which had been obtained for the artist's paintings, quoted in French francs. It appeared that our print may be quite valuable! But in the event we reached neither Amsterdam nor London, as this episode explains.

The following morning, being well satisfied with our visit to Epinal, we prepared to drive on. Bondo's brakes were completely ineffective! What luck that this had not happened on the road. We walked across the river by the footbridge that led to the industrial area which we had noticed when we drove in, and were directed to General Motors garage. Very much later in the morning they sent a young mechanic who immediately diagnosed a faulty brake cylinder. He suggested that we drive very carefully to the garage using the hand-brake if necessary. It was quite a frightening experience crossing the long very heavily trafficked bridge across the river.

After waiting most of the day in the garage yard the patron finally appeared and took over. He had the vehicle jacked up, tightened some screws and refilled with brake fluid and after charging a disgusting fee told us we could drive on.

By now it was too late in the day to "drive on" so we returned to the car park for the night. Next morning – again no brakes and a puddle of brake fluid on the ground!

We drove back to the garage. We stupidly thought we must return to the G.M. garage as they would be the agents for our parts. The Patron was furious – he shouted at us in rapid French of which we could not understand a word of course, as though it was our fault. He showed no remorse for the fact that he had endangered our lives by telling us to drive on.

He thought he would be doing us the greatest favour to try and order the part either from Nancy or Paris. He commanded us to remove ourselves on to a rather dirty, unpalatable parking area on the busy street adjoining the garage. Neither he nor his two female office staff offered us any help, let alone kindness. We had to ask permission to use their facilities, this granted so resentfully that we were made to feel uncomfortable whenever we needed to use those facilities.

The days passed. Each time we asked they answered curtly that they were trying to locate the parts (no information was ever volunteered). We began to wonder whether they were making any serious attempts. When we suggested they phone to Switzerland or allow us to do so, they refused and told us to phone from the post office in town – a long walk away.

The young mechanic, who at least was kind and polite, removed our back wheel and the brake cylinder and left us balancing precariously on three wheels supported by a very flimsy jack. He opined the thought that the part might arrive from Paris on Friday's train. We felt insecure both physically and mentally. Now we were absolutely trapped and at their mercy. We became furious and frustrated. The traffic passing us day and night was unbearable. We could not take the risk of abandoning Bondo to stay in an hotel as surely she would have been broken into and looted in that scruffy area. At one point a woman from the house opposite came out to tell us it was not a caravan camp. She saw our dilemma but offered neither sympathy nor help, except to inform us that the garage patron was a bad man – a fact we already knew to our cost.

Friday came – there was no part. The garage did not operate on Saturdays and Sundays, and Monday was Bastille Day. So we decided that we would go to Switzerland ourselves to try to obtain the part. We took the worn part from the mechanic as a sample. So on Monday morning we boarded a train to Basle, a journey of many hours because it entailed a change of trains and lengthy wait. We knew the G.M. agents in Basle from a previous repair. We duly arrived and they were charming, spoke English and immediately phoned the brake-cylinder specialists who, within a quarter of an hour had sent a car to fetch our sample. We were shown into a waiting room with a kiosk where we could order coffee and something to eat – we needed it. Before we had even finished our refreshments they came to tell us that the part was unavailable in Basle, but that they had ordered it from Zurich and it would arrive next day. They phoned and booked us in a reasonably priced hotel and sent us into town with one of their staff. How we enjoyed the Rheinblik Hotel in a front room overlooking the Rhine. So much so that we stayed an extra night.

How happy we were to finally close that Epinal chapter. We did not have the nerve to continue our long journey to Britain and were, in any case, too late for our appointment in Holland. So we satisfied ourselves with a visit to the Vosges and compensated ourselves by leaving Bondo at a small country railway station and taking a train to Paris for a weekend.

Incidentally the new part was stamped: MADE IN PARIS!

*

A Tap on the Shoulder

After a wonderful sojourn in Norway as described in the previous chapter, which, however, was not without its problems – personal health, recurring battery rundown and consistently bad weather – we were, none the less, reluctant to leave that beautiful uncluttered country we had come to love. We dreaded the long journey southward, especially through Germany, as the prospect of driving through the large cities of the industrialised Ruhr was not enticing. We had discussed this with a German cyclist whom we had met en route on his way down from Nordkapp, sporting a pair of reindeer antlers on his handle-bars. He told us how he himself was dreading this part of his long journey to his home in southern Germany. "There is no alternative for you but to travel on the autobahn," he said, "as the large industrial towns of northern Germany run into one another and finding one's way in and out of them would prove to be a nightmare."

Motorways are anathema to us anyway in our slow moving Bondo with the fast-moving vehicles flashing past us – and we understand that German autobahn traffic is the fastest in the world. Bondo is inclined to sway in the wind generated by big lorries.

The few hours crossing from Larvik in southern Norway to Frederickshavn on the north of Jutland island of Denmark transported us to quite another world of soft, rolling, white sand dunes along the coast where we lay warming ourselves in the sunshine. Denmark has a flat, gentle, cultivated landscape – so great a contrast to the dramatic, rocky, mountainous country we had just left with its fast-flowing rivers and tumbling cascades, its numerous fjords and lakes, its thickly forested mountain sides topped with great glaciers.

We tarried in Denmark's pleasant towns. In Aalborg, enjoying its beautifully designed art museum, and in Arhus we visited the 'old town' where examples of Denmark's traditional half-timbered buildings – private and public, shops and workshops, in cobbled streets, and even an old water-mill on a flowing river, had been re-assembled as an 'old town'.

We crossed from Jutland to Funen Island on one of the two dramatically long bridges; visited Middlefart, one of Denmark's oldest towns and then on to Odense where we spent a nostalgic time being reminded of Hans Christian Andersen's wonderful fairy tales – browsing through the items in the museum in the home of his birth to which he often returned during his lifetime. The house and the street have been preserved as it was in his day. We returned to Bondo armed with a copy of some of the fairy tales and to spend the night on the car park adjoining the city park.

We went to bed rather sad and depressed as we had witnessed a little tragedy while walking in the park during the evening. We had been admiring two small ducks and their single little duckling swimming in the pond when we suddenly became aware of a commotion and saw a large cat with something in its mouth slinking away from the water's edge and disappearing into the bushes. There were pathetic quacks from the ducks and desperate swimming back and forth, back and forth searching for their little duckling. We went to where we had seen the cat disappear, but it was quite impossible to see anything in the thick dark bushes. There was nothing we could do to help.

It was difficult to fall asleep thinking of the sad incident we had just witnessed, wondering what fairy story Hans Andersen would have made of the incident; and worrying about our impending journey.

During the night we both woke simultaneously, as though someone had tapped us on the shoulder. We sat up in bed and declared to one another that we would not go back to Switzerland southwards through Germany – we would have to find another way.

After an early breakfast we studied our maps and decided we would go west the 137 kilometres (eighty-five miles) to Esjberg and take the ferry to England. We retraced our route across the bridge back into Jutland, arriving at Esjberg in the late afternoon.

Next morning, with a strange sense of relief, we crossed the Channel to Harwich – we could not have chosen a more illogical route to return to Switzerland!

On arrival in Britain it is necessary to have an MOT (roadworthy certificate). We were directed to a recommended garage which agreed to take Bondo the next day. We spent a windy night on the open common overlooking the sea, having chased one of our mats being blown by the gale across the common.

First thing next morning we delivered Bondo to the garage and took a train to spend the day in London. We returned to the garage expecting to drive on, only to be told that they could not possibly issue a certificate of roadworthiness as Bondo's brakes and steering were seriously faulty and that it would be extremely dangerous to drive any distance under those conditions. We looked at each other– it was that tap on the shoulder that night in Odense– was it our Guardian Angel? We could only speculate on what might have happened on the long journey with the speeding traffic on the autobahns of Germany.

*

If the reader should wonder when or whether our battery problem was ever solved – yes, it was when we fell upon the Lucas factory after finally leaving Harwich. The trouble was a short in the interior wiring of Bondo. We had been asked by every garage whether we had perhaps left our interior lights on – our reply always was that we *never* ever used them so as to avoid running the battery down. Why did none of those garages bother to check the interior wiring?

*

Finding our Blue Bird (with Apologies to Maeterlink)

Bondo's health had been a matter of concern for some time. We had trailed from one garage to another, but her condition deteriorated seriously.

One Sunday, when we were expected for lunch with our cousins on the Jura, Bondo struggled on the very first incline. She smoked alarmingly, spluttered and threatened to peter out, so we left her at one of the stations and went up the mountain by train.

The next day we visited several garages. None were prepared to undertake repairs on such an old vehicle. Spares were unavailable in Switzerland, so they told us. We were in deep despair as the prospect of life without Bondo was inconceivable.

We contemplated shipping her to Britain. Although we were rather shocked to learn, on inquiries, what it would cost we nevertheless wrote an express letter to the Bedford factory stating our problems and asking their advice. We still await their reply years later!

At the same time we wrote to a friend in England who was connected with the motor business. He replied that the only advice he had received was that we should scrap Bondo and buy another caravan. Even if we could afford to do so *they* did not understand that there could be no replacement of *our* Bondo. None of the new motor-caravans we had ever seen could offer the same comfort.

We limped back to the village where Bondo spends her winters not knowing what to do. We asked the owner of Bondo's shed whether he knew of a reliable garage.

"Yes, the garage which I patronise in the next village only three kilometres from here."

Léonce, the garage owner, examined Bondo. What she needs, we understood (he spoke only French) is a complete overhaul of the engine. He disappeared into his office... then he came back to tell us that the reconditioning experts near Lausanne would undertake the job, would fetch the engine within the next couple of days and return it within a week.

Ten days later (we had spent the time at Denise's mobile home on the lake) we returned to the garage. Léonce had reinstalled the engine and Bondo was given a new lease of life.

Admittedly communication is somewhat difficult, but with the help of our illustrated Bedford manual and dictionary with French motor terms and lots of fun and goodwill we make ourselves understood – Léonce has since then given Bondo his loving care because, as he says with his characteristic mischievous smile, *"J'ai amour de Bondo Bedford."*

He even fetches Bondo from her winter shed where we had been wont to fetch her ourselves for so many years and always encountered problems in getting her engine started. Now she is given a roadworthy check-up and service for our arrival in the spring by postal-bus, a half-hour journey through several villages, from the railway station to the garage at the end of the village where we are welcomed by Léonce, his friendly black Alsatian dog, Falcon, and Bondo rearing to go.

So here, within three kilometres of Bondo's winter home we had found our Blue Bird.

Rural Ramblings

We are often asked how is it possible to spend so long in a motor-caravan. Over the years we have lived in Bondo for an average of four months each summer. It is not a question we can answer in a few words. It is even a question we have to ask ourselves – why indeed? Is it because it takes us so long to get from here to there? A journey that normally takes so many hours takes us that number of days or even weeks. Basically it is because there is no fixed time for us to be either here or there. We enjoy the simple life and both have an abiding love of the countryside and an absorbing interest in farming (we spent the greater part of our childhood on an African farm).

For instance, it was somehow special to meet Friesland cattle in Friesland, hundreds and hundreds of them in the flat fields of Holland, because we kept Frieslands on our farm. We were interested to see cows machine-milked in the field there, and of course stopped to watch and chat to the farmer in our best Afrikaans (we do not know how much he understood). The cows were tethered in a circle facing inwards, the milking machine brought to the field mounted on a flat cart drawn by a tractor. We were rewarded for our interest with a generous helping of fresh warm milk. The farmer refused to accept payment.

In Ireland, the farmer milked by hand direct into our container – what a reminder of our childhood days of fresh, warm, frothy milk. Fresh, unpasteurised milk is an important part of our diet in Switzerland. In the country we go to the depots at the hours when they open to receive milk from the farmers who bring their ten-gallon cans by tractor, by van, in the boots of their cars or on hand-carts. We have even seen children bringing cans on a little cart drawn by a dog.

Very early on in our travels with Bondo, when we arrived in Switzerland for the first time, we were to learn of the status of the cow in that country. Walking towards a village we were puzzled to find that traffic in both directions was at a complete standstill – cars, lorries, caravans. The reason – a few cows, on their own, crossing the road at a very leisurely, dignified pace – one even stopped in the middle of the road to gaze benignly at the vehicles – "The queen goes before!" We followed one of the cows up a side street. She approached a house, stopped at the front door and mooed to announce her arrival, went to the fountain for a drink and then walked to the back of the house and entered her barn.

Our lives in Bondo are very much involved with cows. Each Swiss district has its own traditional breed. We cannot but love them when they gaze at us with that calm, relaxed expression from under their long eyelashes. When we have stayed at small campsites we always park at the very edge of the camp, invariably adjoining a field where cows graze, so they become our nearest neighbours. On our mountain walks on the alpages above the tree lines, where cattle spend their summers, we always encounter them. On one occasion, while we were having our picnic lunch, a cow came up to us and licked Do's face. Whilst walking among them heifers so often come up to us and suck our hands. We love the clanging of their huge bells echoing in the stillness of the mountains on the alpages and the sounds of their bells day and night when we live in the valleys. However, we do have our favourites – the mushroom coloured cows of the Valais and Uri with their soft, velvet coats, large ears and long cream-coloured eyelashes.

In all the Alpine countries that we have visited the cattle are taken high into the mountains in the spring, where they remain all summer. On our climbs and walks we reach the isolated summer stables, sometimes for help when we are not sure of the path or to buy milk for our picnic lunch, or cheese to eat and take home. The farmer cuts about a kilogram for us from the large round forms which he releases from the presses.

From these remote summer farms, of course, they cannot deliver milk daily, so they make cheeses which they carry on their backs down steep mountain paths, or the cheeses are swung down the mountain on a winch or on small rough wooden cable cars. We have ascended and descended in some of these, which are operated by one of the old villagers, whom one has to call for at his home when one wants to go up.

On one occasion, on our arrival at the top, we followed a very steep rough path which led through a deep valley, which fell away hundreds of feet below us in a thickly-forested cleft. We eventually arrived at the end of the valley to an open area above the tree-line and came to two deserted summer farms. Deserted because it was already so late in the season. When we arrived back at the top of the cable we rang the phone, as instructed, and were told to wait seated in the cab. A bell rings and we are off, swinging in the air above the forested mountain.

How we love to watch the parade of the cows when they come down from the mountains in the autumn, wearing enormous bells hanging from their decorative leather collars clanging as they walk, their horns garlanded with flowers, the herdsmen dressed in the national costume of the area; the villagers all out in the streets to greet them with clapping and laughter and the children call out in glee as they run along with the parade.

This is a hint for us to prepare to go home, for any day now the cold weather can set in – the alpine herdsmen always know.

In these times of mass production, mechanisation and computerised milking machines, the practicality of the subsidised mountain farmers, with their ten to fifteen cows, is being questioned by economists and those who discuss Switzerland's consideration of entry into the European Common Market. But Switzerland without its mountain farmers and its self-sufficiency in times of stress would make this over-crowded, industrialised, modern world yet a sadder place.

We also love the white cows of the plains of France and I remember waking at dawn in our camp outside the village of Sancergues and seeing a herd of snow-white cows grazing beneath tall poplars half obscured in the mists rising from the stream. Was I awake or was it some dreamlike vision?

The shaggy highland cattle of Scotland are an integral part of the rugged scenery of the Highlands.

The smallest cattle in the world, the Kerry cattle found in Eire are no taller than a great Dane.

I must confess that we were shocked to learn that the black cattle of the Camargue are specifically bred for bullfighting.

*

Horses, of course, are our first loves. We were brought up with them and they were our closest childhood friends.

We cannot pass a field where horses are grazing without stopping to admire them. They usually come to the fence to greet us. We recall those light brown horses, with long cream-coloured manes, of the Inn Valley (on the road from the Tyrol into Switzerland) who invited us, oh, so nostalgically! to stroke their soft velvet noses. How like in colour to the Norwegian fjordlings, but so much slimmer. The latter, as we mention elsewhere as our guests before breakfast, are hardy, broad little horses who pull carts and traps in the summer and, no doubt, sleighs in the winter.

The wild ponies on Dartmoor have roused us when they have rubbed themselves against Bondo during a night spent on those open moors.

Once we spent a couple of days on the lonely *pampa* of the Camargue (swamplands at the delta of the Rhône). We cannot resist quoting some lines from the poem 'Horses of the Camargue' by Roy Campbell (our countryman):

> In the grey wastes of dread,
> The haunt of shattered gulls where nothing moves
> But in a shroud of silence like the dead,
> I heard a sudden harmony of hooves,
> And turning, saw afar
> A hundred snowy horses unconfined,
> The silver runaways of Neptune's car
> Racing, spray-curled, like waves before the wind,
> Sons of the Mistral...
> Theirs is no earthly breed
> Who only haunt the verges of the earth...
>
> Surely the great white breakers gave them birth...
> With white tails smoking free,
> Long streaming manes and arching necks, they show
> Their kinship to their sisters of the sea...

Also on the Camargue, at sunset, a pink cloud appeared out of a pink sky – the flamingos coming home at the end of the day. They landed near us, making their way delicately through the swamp, lifting high their long black legs, their strange elongated heads on their long necks bobbing up and down as they fed. Early in the morning they took off again, their long legs and long necks forming horizontal lines in the sky with their pink and black wings spread out at right angles. The Camargue is the only part of Europe where flamingos are found in the wild.

Outside Caen, where we had slept under trees beside a stream, we awoke to the cloppety-clop of the trotters drawing their two-wheeled racing chariots, practising down the course in the early morning mist. Also in Normandy, at Sainte-Mère-Église we watched champion jumpers practising.

Driving out of Brighton past the racecourse we realised that a race-meeting was taking place, as evidenced by the large number of cars parked at the course – so we decided to go to the races. We lost the pound we bet on a horse, but how worthwhile to watch the proud, impatient, beautiful creatures parading in the paddock and to be part of the excitement of the crowd as the horses thundered down the course.

On a road in Wales we saw temporary signposts directing motorists to CROSS-COUNTRY HORSE TRIALS. We followed the sign to look in and see what it was all about. This proved to be a most enjoyable day for us. The jumps of varying hazards were spaced rather far apart – so we also enjoyed cross-country walking. There were high jumps, wide jumps over ditches; but the most difficult and exciting to watch was the jump over four logs at different heights and angles plus a water-hole.

In a Swiss village, beyond Neuchâtel, we also saw excellent horse-jumping over a variety of obstacles, but the most novel part of these competitions were the horse and carriage events of two and four-in-hand. The skill of the drivers and horses tackling the hazards at terrific speed was most exciting.

*

We left Lucerne late one afternoon as we had tarried longer as usual and drove down the pass into the valley which continues on to the Emmental. It was time to look for somewhere to spend the night before it became too dark. Outside one of the villages was a church and parking area well off the road and facing out across the fields – ideal! We had supper and settled down for a quiet and restful night.

In the morning we were aware of some movement around us, and looking out saw a large pig grovelling in the lush grass, grunting with obvious satisfaction at his new-found freedom. He had probably escaped from his sty! The only other occasion that we saw pigs roaming free, was when climbing down from the Schilthorn, they were grazing with goats on a high mountain farm.

Though pork is in evidence in every butcher shop in Switzerland, pigs are not to be seen – they are kept in closed pigsties. On one occasion while searching to buy fresh milk on a Swiss farm we came upon a long, low building with many windows, each curtained and with lovely flowers in the window boxes – we looked in and there Large Whites lay, an hygienic mass of pinkish coloured amoebae – completely immobile and quite revolting. We burst out laughing when we reminded each other of the pigs on our African farm, somewhat different creatures, wild black swine perpetually jumping the fences of their Heath Robinson sties, built of rough poles and corrugated iron, and rushing off into the veldt with Africans and dogs in hot pursuit. When caught by the back leg, as was the custom, their squeals could be heard for miles around. When pigs had to be moved we tried to transport them separately on a wheelbarrow, held down by three Africans. The screeching and squeaking was deafening. Some of our sows had no maternal instincts. They rolled on their piglets, squashing them into the cold mud in wet weather so that the pathetic little squealing creatures had to be rescued and brought home to the kitchen, wrapped in a blanket and put into the open oven to be dried and warmed. Certainly our pigs were much more fun!

*

On the Isle of Skye we watched sheep being sheared in the fields. A young man of fine physique was shearing in a small pen constructed of wooden poles. An old man brought the sheep to the shearer and another old man, with pipe between his teeth, was rolling and packing the wool into hessian sacks. A lovely black and white sheep dog was also on hand, but he found time to be very friendly towards us.

The shearer told us that he shears two hundred and thirty sheep per day. Lynn timed him – two in three and a half minutes. He said that he works in Australia and New Zealand during their shearing seasons. How expert he was and how quiet and patient the sheep. We remembered sheep-shearing on our African farm. It took two Africans to hold the frightened, struggling animal down while the shearer cut the wool away with hand-clippers, often wounding the poor sheep when it struggled.

We attended sheep-dog trials in Scotland to watch the remarkable interaction between man, dog and sheep. Sheep-dog trials are competitions where the best dog wins a prize for its expertise in handling the flock.

From a distance, the shepherd calls out his instructions or whistles – the dog hesitates for a moment, pricks up his ears, wags his tail and then gets on with the task. The dog rounds up the sheep in the field, manoeuvres them through a narrow gate, guides them across the field towards a sheep pen, then herds them through a narrow entrance. I would say it is a form of art.

And so there is never a dull moment – so many of these moments and days are unplanned and unexpected.

*

We have heard the sound of the electric saws echoing through the forests and witnessed the drama of the great forest giants crashing down. We have seen how the logs, attached to cables, are swung across deep valleys to the mountain roads for their transport to the saw-mills in the valley below. It is interesting to watch the enormous moving blades cutting the logs into boards.

In Switzerland we have witnessed how one man, on his own, drives his lorry with its crane, loads a pile of large logs and drives off. In any other country the same job would require at least three men.

Tiny, sophisticated farm machinery is used on the small mountain farms in the Alps. Minute tractors draw the mowers and rotary hay dryers and the roller attachment that loads the hay on to a wagon.

But there is still work done by the old methods – drying hay by pitching it with long-pronged wooden forks. Not only do we watch whole families haymaking in the summer, but we have also joined them.

The scythe is still very much in use on slopes too steep even for the tiniest mowers. It is interesting to observe the different methods of stacking and drying hay in different shapes of stacks – tall, thin, fat or short on cleverly constructed wooden stakes, each country with its own traditional method. In Norway, Ticino and Austria the hay is hung out to dry on wire fences, like washing, in long parallel rows, picturesque on the hillsides.

On the large flat farms in France, Denmark and England, enormous machines roll wheat chaff into large roly-polys which are wrapped in plastic and left in the field instead of being stored in sheds. This is now normal practice which we have seen in Norway and Switzerland as well. We have also seen them stacked forming a long pipe. On Swedish wheat-fields we saw the largest combines we have ever seen.

Instead of the back-breaking method of lifting potatoes, potato harvesters carry six sorters, usually women, who ride on a platform on the mechanical digger as it is drawn by a tractor along the rows. There has been much laughter when we have offered to help and been invited aboard.

In Ireland the work of peat cutting is still done by hand. A peat-cutter at work told us that this work is a great strain on the heart and that peat-cutters die young.

*

Grape Harvest

Our dearest Swiss friends are country folk. Their fine old farmhouse, in a village in the Vaud, stands atop the Vully hills above its vineyards which drop down a slope that overlooks the fertile agricultural lands of the Broye Valley.

On fine summer evenings the family entertains friends and customers beneath a vine pergola, filling and refilling glasses with the fine wines of their cellars. After dark or on dull days we sit on low stools round a rough log table in the cellar, where our glasses are filled directly from taps in the huge oak vats. Hard cheese is served, sliced by passing it over a blade set in a wooden board.

The end of the grape harvest season is a very special event shared by family and friends with the pickers, village neighbours and growers in neighbouring villages who sell their crops to the winery. We have the honour to help with the picking and to share in the event.

The baskets of grapes are carried from the vineyards and tipped into large wooden tanks, housed in a shed behind the house where the first fermentation takes place. Grapes from surrounding vineyards arrive on flat tractor-drawn wagons, but before being tipped into the tanks are weighed and registered in the name of each grower.

In the same shed is the wine press. A long modern machine with rollers presses the grapes, which have been transferred from the tanks, and the juice is filtered through a perforated metal sheet surrounding the roller and drops into a trough, into which we are invited to dip our glasses for a drink of grape juice.

From the trough the juice flows through a pipe to the back porch of the house into a tank from which it is pumped to be refined by passing through a series of cloth filters and from there again pumped into the huge oakwood vats in the cellar where the wine will then mature.

After the last of the season's grapes have been brought to the winery all concerned are invited to a party on the upper floor of the shed where a long table is set for a meal and plenty of last year's wine to go with it. But first, the 'loving cup' is passed round.

The next evening we dined with the family, a culinary delight of fresh mushrooms and walnuts which we had helped to gather. Also at the meal was Auntie, aged eighty-five, who, while we were gathering mushrooms and walnuts, was up a ladder in the apple orchard picking the fruit.

We retired, quite enjoying the novelty of sleeping under a roof as our hostess, as always, refused to allow us to sleep 'at home' out there in the yard where Bondo was parked. After drinking so much wine we slept very soundly.

Next morning we departed, loaded by our hosts with gifts of grapes, fresh vegetables and berries, bottles of wine and a cherry tart, a traditional seasonal dish. How lucky we are and how much we appreciate such warm hospitality and generosity from these Swiss friends.

*

If we thought that Bondo was our 'retirement home' we were very much mistaken because we have become vineyard workers, learning a new job, helping to trim the vines, thinning out the excessive new growth, so as to concentrate all the strength on the bunches of developing grapes which will eventually become the wine of next year's vintage. This is all part of our 'adoption' by our dear Swiss friends *la famille* Vigneronne of the famous Vully wines.

Hot work in a Swiss summer heat wave... But oh! so amply rewarded at the end of the day with a refreshing swim at the lakeside chalet, and a grilled lake-fish supper cooked on the outdoor grill and washed down by generous, and I may add, excessive quantities of good Vully wine. We live in Bondo in the chalet garden, beneath an enormous oak and tall poplars and the willows that shed their fluffy seeds around us like falling snow.

As the sun drops it casts a brilliant path across the lake and then disappears behind the Jura mountains, which become a hazy navy-blue backdrop to the lake, reflecting in its tranquil waters the brilliance of changing colours of the sky and clouds above.

The chalet is almost at the end of a very narrow one kilometre length dirt road that serves the chalets along the shores of the lake. It has its own tiny beach approached through a tunnel of bush and reeds. We call it 'Ginette's Shangri La', which we have the privilege to share.

These chalets were built long before these south-eastern shores of Lake Neuchâtel were declared a nature reserve, and no further development permitted. The lake shore with its swamps and thick reeds is a bird sanctuary and breeding grounds for many hundreds of species of water birds, among them swans.

The vineyard is a short drive away, passing through a varicoloured patchwork of rich farmlands and forests to the Vully slopes and their vineyards.

Bondo awaits us on the road above the vines and is viewed with curiosity, no doubt, by the village farmers passing up and down the road on their tractors drawing various types of farm implements.

On our second day in the vineyards we have become almost professional. A very slight breeze and some cloud cover eases our work and is indicative of an impending storm. The storm broke with strong winds and driving rain. After about an hour it was all over. We returned to the lake – now a wild sea. The waves were breaking on our little beach and rushing up over the sand, depositing logs and branches on the shore.

We spent the mornings at the lake and went to work each afternoon, returning to the chalet, stopping en route in the cool of the forest to rest.

By the end of the week we completed our share of the work. We reviewed with pride the beauty of a well-trimmed vineyard, every vine equal in height, neatly secured to its stake, the parallel lush green rows merging in perspective down the slope.

Beyond the valley below, with its patchwork of fields, and half-hidden behind a thick forest of poplars, can be seen the glimmering waters of Lake Morat (Murten) – on the far distant horizon the pale misty outline of the Alps.

Our Home Towns

Estavayer-le-Lac

There are certain small towns and villages in which we have come to feel completely at home, where there is a parking area which provides several basic essentials – privacy and anonymity, silence (i.e. well away from the sound of traffic), no disturbing lights at night, shade when it is hot and protection from cold and wind; above all, of course, adequate facilities, telephone and shops within easy walking distance for our daily requirements.

Estavayer-le-Lac provides us with all the above very special comforts and in particular on our spring arrival and autumn departure. It is within ten kilometres of Bondo's winter home and her own very special garage in a nearby village. Our closest friends live in the area, convenient to visit and for us to entertain.

The parking is at the lake, the town on the rise above; the parking serves the very large yachting harbour and the pier for the lake steamers on Lake Neuchâtel. It has all the above facilities plus hot and cold water day and night and two sets of facilities. It has considerable flexibility in that it is large enough to move house to suit the weather and the mood. On weekends and holidays we can move to greater privacy in the parking bay between the gardens where we are hidden by trees.

We have a special love for this medieval walled town to which we look up from 'our home' to the towers of its château, fine church steeple floodlit on summer nights and its attractive old houses. We enjoy our own comings and goings up the steep, winding cobbled streets and stairways between the lovely old houses and covered walkways to do our shopping, use the post office, banks and laundry (specially convenient for our final washing) and even the travel agency to book our passage home.

Our parking on the lake-side at Estavayer-le-Lac

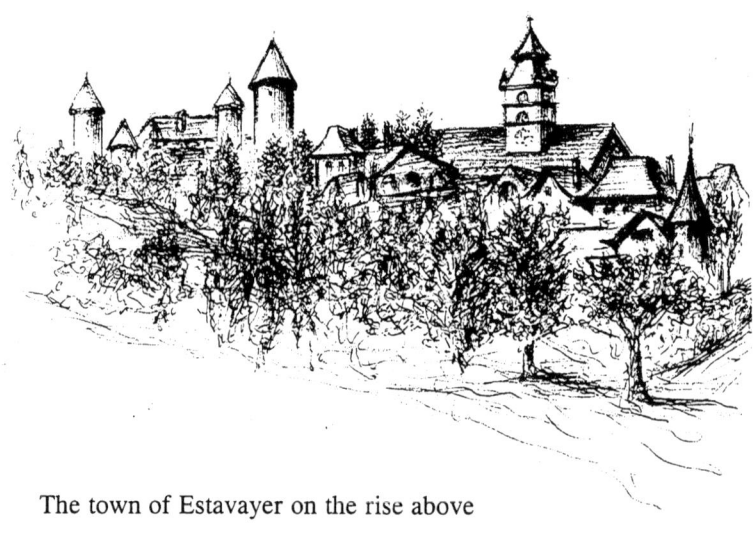

The town of Estavayer on the rise above

We love the gentility and politeness of the people. That warm *"bon jour, madame"* – *"service, madame"*. They recognise us after all these years but we presume that they do not guess that we actually live on their car park.

The parking area is surrounded by tall poplars and willows and is open to the lake. Our 'gardens' are beautifully kept with gorgeous rose bushes, decorative trees and rolling lawns. The bird life is special. There are thousands of lake gulls, many varieties of ducks and so many swans. We count as many as fifty swans at a time in the autumn. This side of the lake is a bird sanctuary.

The view west across the lake takes in the Jura mountain range, behind which the sun drops in a brilliance of colour setting the lake afire. On our evening walks along the pier, jutting out into the lake, we watch and feed the gulls, ducks and swans which in their masses fight for the pieces of bread we throw to them. We watch the graceful sailing boats as they glide across the reflection of the setting sun.

*

Avenches

We have another convenient 'home' at Avenches, at one time the Roman Capital of Helvetia. We go there regularly to attend the 'spectacles' which are staged in the Roman amphitheatre.

We also use this 'home' at other times when in the area. Our gas depot for refilling our cooking gas containers is in a nearby village and the caravan shop where we sometimes require purchases is in this town's industrial area. Avenches is also conveniently near the homes of two sets of friends.

The parking area, not very large, is most conveniently situated adjoining the amphitheatre on one side, on another side the outer walls of the château which separates us from the town centre, the third side adjoins the small town's stately home and the fourth side drops down into the Broye Valley overlooking the Vully hills and beyond to the Jura. Its ancient trimmed lime trees afford us shade and privacy.

When we come specially to attend performances we arrive early to select our most convenient 'plot', purchase our tickets, dress and dine and after the performance we are already 'at home' for the night.

We have lost our special site below La Bâtiaz in Martigny, one of
our favourite towns, where a block of modern flats now occupies
'our' site.

Living in the shadow of the Château at Avenches

We do enjoy the historic pageantry at which the Swiss excel and in 1991 there were very special performances depicting the seven-hundredth year of the Swiss Confederation, with a marvellous firework display.

Here too the small medieval town is of interest and the Roman remains in the area around are proof of how large a city Aventicum was in Roman times.

*

Langnau

Langnau is of particular interest to us as a half-way house on our way to and from Central Switzerland. It is a market town which serves the rich farming district of the Emmental, famous for its cheeses of that name.

The market square is in the centre of the town, surrounded by magnificent old trees. When not occupied as a market the square becomes a car park in addition to the parking area on either side. We usually arrive after business hours so have the pick of the parking places. If however there is a NO PARKING sign displayed on the square we know that we must park on the outer extension. The facilities are five-star, hygienically and aesthetically with pink floral tiling on walls and floor.

On one occasion as we woke in the early morning, the market folks had already arrived and were packing out and setting up long trestle tables for laying out their products for sale. They greeted us with friendly smiles. What an opportunity we had to buy fresh farm products – fruit, vegetables, home-made jams and delicious cheeses.

On another occasion someone knocked on our window in the early morning and asked us to move further back in the parking area behind us. We were surprised to see large numbers of cows arriving, some herded and others brought in lorries from which they descended down ramps. There was much mooing of cows and shouting by herdsmen as the cows were tethered face to face on iron railings on both sides of the square. The farmers soothed nervous cows and some were busy grooming them. Municipal workers with jet hoses were keeping the area clean (how we always respect the Swiss for their cleanliness).

Enormous bells attached to decorative leather collars, which are the symbols of a cow's worth, were stacked under a large tree.

Although it had been our intention to drive on after breakfast we decided to stay on to watch the proceedings. As each cow was led forward she was thoroughly examined by two evaluators, one of whom wrote details on a large pad. At this rate the examination of about sixty cows would take hours. No one seemed to be in any hurry – buyers and sellers were chatting and joking. The farmers' children were also lending a hand, presumably having a day off from school. Curious as we were to see how the actual sales are conducted we decided not to wait.

The next time we arrived after hours on a Friday. The market square was almost empty. After dinner, at about eight o'clock, cars arrived one after another taking up every parking space. We presumed that some entertainment was on in town, so decided to investigate. To our surprise we found all the shops open. It appears that they always open on Fridays until 9.30 p.m. to allow the busy farmers time to come to town to shop.

Incidentally this little town has the widest variety of goods that can be found anywhere and most attractively displayed. So we joined the shoppers, examined the bargain baskets outside the shoe store and went inside.

Never before have we seen so many shoes, shelf after shelf reaching to the ceiling, all displayed. Lynn made a very successful purchase.

In a hardware store we found an item for which we had searched unsuccessfully elsewhere. Then on to the dairy which we always patronise, with its wide selection of cheeses, beautifully displayed and served by two attractive girls in red uniforms and caps. One spoke excellent English and helped us select cheeses.

We bought our usual fresh unpasteurised milk which is available in dairies and/or milk depots everywhere in Switzerland – an important part of our diet. We also enjoy sour milk and even make our own cottage cheese.

We will postpone our next shopping spree until our next sojourn in Langnau.

*

St Gingolph

We drove into St Gingolph waved through by the Swiss customs officials and, after crossing the bridge waved through again by the French customs officials. No problem – Bondo is at least a member of the European Union.

We decided to take a break here from the heavy traffic on the road we had come along (only a two-lane road carries all the traffic between Switzerland and France on this side of the lake). We turned off at the first convenient road that led down the hill to the lake. How beautiful and how peaceful!

We eventually found excellent private parking under some trees in front of an unoccupied and, it seemed, long abandoned café. There were views across the lake to Montreux and Vevey and in the far distance the snow-covered peaks of the Vaudois Alps. Being out-of-season there was scarcely anyone around, only the locals quietly fishing off the pier. Having found this lovely 'plot' we decided to stay and become acquainted with this unique little town where it was possible to live in two countries at the same time, and perhaps climb the mountains above.

A narrow river, cascading its way down from the mountains to the lake below runs through the town and is the frontier between Switzerland and France. Several small bridges join the two countries.

The peace of the little town has been spoilt by the roar of enormous pantechnicons with their trailers and the massive traffic of cars and trucks as they rumble through the narrow main street by day and by night. Pedestrians have to walk in single file on pavements narrowed to accommodate the heavy traffic.

The French and Swiss cross back and forth over the bridge to shop on either side and in either currency, in French shops with Swiss currency to advantage. Most of the shops are in France. Everything is duplicated – the town Communes, churches, post-offices, schools, public telephones and even public toilets (the latter on the Swiss side more modern and more acceptable).

St Gingolph once shared a common history. Both halves were part of the French Department of Savoie, the Valais becoming part of the Swiss Federation only in 1815. During the terrible years of World War Two the connection was completely severed – but it seems not in spirit.

The sad history of French St Gingolph is poignantly illustrated at the Place Charles de Gaulle – Monument of the Fusiliers. Below the statue of a soldier falling are the names of those who fell in France's wars – the Franco-Prussian War, the First and Second World Wars – many of the same family names are repeated. On one wall is a bronze relief of the head of Charles de Gaulle with the dates of his birth and death and below it a framed copy of his manifesto (issued in London) calling upon the French to resist. It seems that many in St Gingolph answered his call. Carved on grey stone are the names of those who were shot on this square – hence the name Monument to the Fusiliers – and those who were captured and never returned.

A caption under the photograph of the burning town reads "…by a ruthless and brutal enemy – 23 July 1944". On another grey stone is carved the name of the Swiss General and his unit: "In grateful thanks for kind assistance throughout those dreadful years."

The Château on the Swiss side, once the home of the Duc de Savoie, now houses on its lower floors the local school and on the upper floor an exhibition of brilliantly constructed model ships which tells the story of St Gingolph as one of the most important harbours serving the transport of cargo and passengers across Western Europe's largest internal waterway. Models of boats from the most primitive wooden craft with a single square sail to cargo vessels, still in use early in this century, are made to scale and meticulously constructed down to the smallest details, showing the goods aboard either in bulk or in sacks, timber in logs or in planks, models of sheep and cattle, little figurines of the crew at work, even the little wheelbarrows they used for loading and unloading, also smartly dressed passengers.

Today on the lake there are the passenger services, mostly for tourists, barges carrying sand from the dredgers at river mouths, small fishing boats and pleasure craft that sail silently on the lake. What a sad change! Road and rail traffic has turned our world into the hell it now is with traffic roaring and rumbling through the once lovely towns and villages that surround the lake.

Happily one can escape down the hill to the lake shore to the silence of lake waters lapping, the cries of the gulls as they circle above the little fishing boats when the nets are drawn in – and the ever patient fishermen on the edge of the pier hour after hour dropping their lines into the lake optimistically hoping for a catch. We watch fascinated, sharing their patience and their optimism.

The next day the weather deteriorated. While we were out we were caught in a heavy downpour and had to take shelter. When we finally reached 'home' the red storm-warning lights flashing from across the lake confirmed that bad weather could be expected. The wind came up lashing the water against the rocks and rolling great big black clouds over the lake obliterating the scene beyond in a curtain of rain. The fishermen had abandoned their posts on the pier and it was obvious that we too would be abandoning our intention to climb the mountain. No point even to plan to move on. Cosily 'at home' we could watch the drama of the storm, a good excuse to stay on, away from traffic on the roads in the peace of the lake front. When our kind French neighbours, who lived next door secluded from us in a walled garden, welcomed us and invited us to stay as long as we wished we felt very comfortable. The area was quite deserted. During the next days the bad weather persisted and we only managed short strolls along the shore or across the little bridge to watch the now raging river and on to the Swiss side with its two smart restaurants attached to small hotels. Parking for clients only!

And so we can add St Gingolph – French and Swiss – to our home towns.

Encounters

Bondo Meets her Twin

As we were driving in Wales early one evening we suddenly spied Bondo's twin parked on a village car park. Of course we immediately drew in beside her – even the curtains were identical, the only difference being that Bondo has a green band round her waist while the twin sported a maroon coloured band, therefore they could not be described as identical twins, just twins. Bondo's twins are few and far between as Bondo is among the last of her not very prolific line.

The owners were not at home, so we waited. Eventually a young couple arrived and of course warm greetings were exchanged and we invited them in for drinks. They told us that Bondo's twin was their only home. He was a travelling salesman, representing hotel advertising, and his wife had retired from teaching to keep house in their mobile home.

We all spent the night together in a beautiful valley after leaving the car park in convoy. Bondo slept beside her twin, to whom she paid a tearful farewell next morning – it was raining!

*

Puma, *Frère à* Bondo

While camping for several days on the river bank outside the village of Moghegno in the Valle Maggia, Do took a walk one morning in the forest within a stone's throw of our 'home' where she came upon a middle-aged couple sitting on low stools outside their little tent having a drink. They waved to her and being a friendly pair of French-speaking Swiss called out to her to join them for a drink. Do expected fruit juice – but no, it was whisky. Subsequently they came to dinner with us and arrived with their bottle of whisky and we spent a giggly evening together.

George did not speak a word of English, although his father, at the age of about twelve years, emigrated to Switzerland with his parents from Scotland. George's grandfather came to Switzerland as Thomas Cook & Son's representative. George has, however, inherited the Scots' love of whisky.

This encounter was the beginning of a friendship of many years. They live in a village in the Vaud not far from our headquarters and invited us to visit them when we returned to the area.

Claire-Marie is a journalist and regular contributor of humorous articles to a women's magazine. She has also written a novel since we first met, but we have not yet been able to ascertain whether it has been published. She is very eccentric, full of the joie de vivre, dresses like a teenager and George gazes in adoration. He is her second husband, and paints pleasing landscapes.

Their tiny flat is overcrowded with knickknacks and paintings by past and present husbands. On our first visit we were treated to an exotic lunch, stayed on into the evening hours, danced and laughed together in their tiny lounge with very little common language. Claire-Marie always insists on speaking English which is worse than my French.

However, they were so impressed with Bondo that within a couple of years they acquired a van, which George himself fitted up as a very comfortable and colourful caravan for living in and they now travel everywhere with her, and their cat, Radibou, always accompanies them and a special shelf has been installed as her bed. Puma is always referred to as brother to Bondo.

Every summer we meet them at their home and together Bondo and Puma set off in convoy to a forest in the vicinity where we all drink whisky while George grills the sausages for supper on his open-air barbecue, with a glass of whisky near at hand.

At the end of an evening of lots of laughter and little serious conversation, due to language barriers, Claire-Marie and George go home while we stay and spend the night in the forest. Sometimes they also stay the night in the forest with us, but depart at dawn in time for George to get to work in Lausanne.

On one occasion we were on our way to visit them when Bondo broke down, some fifty miles away. We phoned to tell them that we were forced to spend the weekend behind a garage. The immediate response was that they would come to us and bring the "*repas*", and so we all drove together in their Puma, leaving Bondo lonely behind the garage, to a suitable picnic site where we drank whisky as usual while George grilled meat on his open fire, drank his whisky and uttered not a word.

On our next visit to Switzerland we phoned, as usual, to arrange a meeting only to be told by George that Claire-Marie had died. We went to offer our condolences. Poor George, we wept for him and for the end, after fifteen years, of the happy times we had spent together, with Bondo and Puma in the forest of Mézières.

*

A Ghost Story

We had been sightseeing in the fascinating little Somerset town of Dunster with its old octagonal-roofed market place astride the main road of the town and its castle on the hill. We were fascinated by the antiques displayed in its old-fashioned shop windows. It was getting late and with our usual irresponsibility we had no idea where we would sleep that night. We were heading from here to Exmoor and the Lorna Doone country.

We drove up a hill out of the town as the sun was beginning to set. After a few miles we noticed a lay-by at the edge of the forest with huge trees overhanging to form a sort of arbour, very still and rather lonely – no traffic passed along the road. We dined and settled down for the night.

Something awakened me during the night. Rather fearfully I lifted the curtain and peeped out – there was no one around. The dark shadows in the forest looked menacing and the rolling moors opposite with dark clumps of trees mystic and beautiful under the full moon. I felt strangely ill at ease and tense, waiting for a repeat of the sound that had awakened me. The sound of a twig dropping onto the roof was reassuring and so I dropped off to sleep.

As we drove into the village next morning, seeing the milkman we stopped to buy milk for breakfast. He greeted us: "I saw you on the roadside at Cutcombe when I passed by in the early hours. Weren't you afraid?"

"Of what?" I asked, remembering the night.

"Many years ago, in the eighteenth century or thereabouts, a coachman had attended a wedding in the nearby village, got very drunk and on his way home the coach overturned and he was killed on the very spot where you were parked. Every full moon night, it is said, he drives down the road again!" It gave us the creeps. Maybe I had just missed seeing the runaway coach and horses. We bought a book on local ghost stories that was displayed in the village shop. We ought to know what to expect in this district of ghostly legends!

*

A Moving Encounter

In another delightful Somerset town we spent several days having car repairs, visiting friends, attending a theatre performance and sleeping nights in the theatre car park. We had driven into a park for afternoon tea in Bondo when we espied a pair of wheelchairs driving along a path. They drew up to stop very close together and the occupants put their arms round one another and started kissing. A few minutes later as they rode past us we greeted them and started a conversation. They told us that they were on a visit from Exeter and that they were engaged to be married – he well in his sixties and she somewhat younger – with such a happy expression. We felt so happy for them to realise that they were able to overcome their disabilities and start a new life together. Of course, we were too polite to ask the extent of their disabilities, for how long they had been disabled and how long their acquaintance. A stirring example of how some people are able to live with and overcome such devastating physical handicaps.

*

Admirable Characters

In Hay-on-Wye, the city of books, we returned 'home' after browsing along the miles of books – how could we choose what to buy if we were not looking for a specific book? In the end we bought a couple of books that were really not exactly treasures, because we could not afford the books we would like to have acquired. We had inquired about selling our second edition of Dickens, the complete set, but they were not interested as our set is no longer in perfect condition – family heirloom, in fact.

However, on the car park we found a couple in a trailer caravan and, of course, got into conversation. They were quite surprised when we told them that we intended spending the night – just there. They were relieved not to have to hunt for a caravan camp and decided to remain as our neighbours for the night. The result, several hours spent together that evening. They are a most interesting and admirable couple. Joan was an adopted child and they in their turn adopted children although they already had a son of their own. They had spent several years in West Africa as missionaries. Joan was now employed by the Prisons Department as Education and Rehabilitation Officer. Bernard was retired from teaching but now very active also in rehabilitation work. In addition they took into their own large home in Nottingham freed prisoners and convicts on parole, whom they helped in so many ways, rehabilitating and finding employment for them.

We were invited to visit them in their home, which we did a few years later, having kept up a correspondence in the meantime. They insisted that we sleep in the house – by then the large home had been sold and they had moved to a small cottage in a village. We were conducted to the bedroom, but somehow we felt that it was not the guest room. Next morning we tackled them on the subject and they admitted that they had given us their bedroom and slept on the convertible couch in the dining-room. Of course, we insisted that we sleep on the couch the next night. What hospitality!

During our stay with them they took us on a wonderful trip round their area, Robin Hood country.

*

A Mother's Dream

And Joy – whom we first met at the Ouchy camp on our very first visit to Lausanne and with whom our friendship has continued all these years. She was also living in a caravan as a member of a travelling dance troupe with which she was a can-can dancer.

Subsequently, she and a partner had their own act with a group of performing dogs which they had trained, entitled 'Cocktail Dogs' with which they toured extensively.

On her return home to England Joy married and had a son late in life. There is a theory that a genius is often the first child of a not so young mother.

Ian, at the age of eleven years certainly showed signs of extraordinary talent as a dancer, playing musical instruments, swimming champion in his age group, and also very clever at school.

After very demanding auditions he was accepted as a junior student at the Birmingham Royal Ballet School. During his first year at the school Ian was chosen to perform with the Company's Christmas production of *The Nutcracker* – traditionally the stepping stone to a child's future career as a premier *danseur* or ballerina.

We followed his progress with interest and looked forward, balletomanes that we are, to seeing Ian perform as a dancer with the Royal Birmingham Ballet Company.

But sadly, little Ian was involved in a motor accident. His left arm was so badly crushed that it became questionable whether he would ever be able to dance again. However, after numerous operations and skin grafts, and his own determination, Ian was accepted as a dancing student at the Arts Educational School at Tring, but as there can be no development of his left arm he has been transferred to the Drama class, as the school said that he is as talented in acting as he is as a dancer.

Nevertheless, he has been chosen yet another Christmas season to dance with the English National Ballet and also to play the part of Puck, the youngest among the school's students.

How bravely Joy, now in poor health, battles to obtain sponsorship for Ian's school fees.

*

The Pringles of the Pyrenees

We left Jaca, the border garrison town of Aragon, in the early morning heading towards the Sompert Pass to cross the Pyrenees into France. Jaca was once the capital of Aragon. We had spent almost a week there having quite by chance arrived in time for their Fiesta honouring their patron saint Santa Orosia. The eleventh-century cathedral is on the Pilgrims' Route to Santiago de Compostela.

We watched a colourful religious procession; folk-dancing in the streets; Mardi Gras characters with huge grotesque masks who teasingly chased the children followed by Ferdinand and Isabella twelve feet tall; lively street musicians whom we followed into each pub. There was also go-cart racing and expert figure skating on the town's ice rink. We lived on a tree-lined avenue outside the Benedictine convent and overlooking the old fortress still being used by the garrison. Having had our fun we left Jaca early and stopped for breakfast on a flat grassy area overlooking a river and the mountains ahead. Another caravan was also parked there some distance from us.

Whilst breakfasting, a knock on our window and an English voice asked whether we had any books to exchange. A friendship ensued and we stayed on until the next day.

The Pringles had been retired for twelve years. Mr Pringle had spent his working life in the British Army serving in many parts of the world – so we understood that this wandering life was what he had been used to. He had converted his caravan into a comfortable home from an old London ambulance which he had purchased and in which they had been living for the past twelve years – they had no other home. They had chosen Spain because the beer and cigarettes are cheap – both of which they consume in large quantities – and also because they can spend the winters in the south of Spain and move up to the Pyrenees for the summer. They had no children, only a nephew in England – their postal address.

We spent an enjoyable twenty-four hours with them, during which time Mr Pringle attempted to correct our smoking exhaust which had blown black smoke over diners on pavement restaurants in Jaca, but without success. He also lent us his powerful radio to listen to the Entebbe drama. We wonder whether they are still living in their ambulance and enjoying the gorgeous Pyrenees in summer.

*

Babes in the Woods

We were in the Basque country of northern Spain. Late one afternoon we reached the top of the pass. The climb was a little more than we had bargained for, trying always to consider Bondo who had just had a tooth pulled (her thermostat) by a friendly camper, an encounter that led to lasting friendship and a visit to them in England. We found an excellent park in a picnic area among tall trees beyond the village of Elgueta, and as it was already nearly 8 p.m. it was time for a night stop. The stark mountains we had been among and viewed through the pinewoods as we climbed the pass were now transparent pink behind the setting sun. The valley fell sharply into a deep enclave backed by pine-covered mountains running up on either side, a foreground to the pink peaks beyond and a rose-tinted sky. We levelled Bondo with some difficulty as the ground was very rough and uneven. We walked to the field on the other side, also dropping away to deep valleys and overlooking a landscape of rolling rounded hills. Way in the distance a patchwork of forest and fields and newly ploughed lands with distant views of minute white walled, red tiled Basque farmhouses dotted the landscape.

Early next morning heavy cloud hung over the valley with high peaks piercing through like a glacial valley landscape. Later in the morning we walked down to the small village with its narrow street and some old houses and the inevitable potted plants. There was a stone church with its square bell tower which dominated the village. There was a covered walk around the church which was fronted by a square of formal garden. We shopped extravagantly and returned to Bondo to lunch sumptuously on minute steak and wine. We had washed up and prepared to drive off when the village children arrived and we eventually conversed by signs to the group of teenage girls. Somehow we were given to understand that in the evening they would be showing a film of their recent Fiesta and invited us to come, and we accepted. Then one of the girls went back to the village and returned with her basque flute which she played and they showed us a few steps of a dance. The leader among them clearly indicated her very strong Basque feelings, not for Spain but for Basque representation at the Olympics.

In the evening they returned to fetch us as promised and we walked with them to the village to the back of the school. We were surrounded by children of all ages and then joined by a few women. Some of the children indicated that they learned English, some French, but when we spoke they did not understand. It was rather embarrassing being stared at and unable to communicate. However one of the girls did know a few words of French and we then gathered that the film had not arrived, so we started back to our woods followed by a large group of the children – we felt like the Pied Piper of Hamelin. The two teenage girls went off to fetch their flutes and when they returned and started to play all the children started to dance – a little shyly at first, but they soon forgot us and then did various folk dances representing agricultural activities. After a while they invited us to join them. They included us in a follow-my-leader type of dance across the grass and between the trees, the boy ahead of me gallantly guiding me away from stones and tree stumps in the grass. They ended the dancing with a grand climax, the music rising to crescendo, somersaulting towards the middle of the circle in a laughing tumbled mass of legs in the air. We were all having fun. It was beginning to get dark among the giant trees, and one by one they came up to us, shook hands and said "*Adieu.*"

The two flautists and the other teenage girls indicated that they wanted to exchange addresses so we invited them in. There were too many of them to be accommodated inside Bondo so the overflow gathered at the front door. Some of the other children who were still around pressed their little noses against the windows all round, curious to see what Bondo looked like inside. We exchanged Spanish, Basque and Hebrew greetings and wrote down names and addresses.

We had been there for thirty hours and were invited to return next year and stay for some days. Then the two flautists played plaintive farewell tunes. Exchanging warm handshakes they slowly withdrew to their village and the stillness closed in around us in the dark forest.

*

Encounter with the Army

An amusing, but very brief encounter took place in the woods belonging to the estate of the Château Chambord in France, where we had settled down for the night.

Sometime during the night lights appeared which passed us. We were not sure what vehicles, but a short time later I suddenly saw some soldiers coming towards us, lit from behind. Two of them jumped down from the bank on to the clearing with rifles held high – a most peculiar sight lit from behind by the strong torch.

Do lay low, as we often do so as not to give away the fact that we are two women alone. The soldiers came up to Bondo and peered in. I said that we wanted to stay the night as we could not find a camp. The soldier replied, "*S'il vous plaît ne faisez pas des feux,*" and wished me "*bon nuit.*"

*

Manoeuvres on the Oberalp

We had come along the Sedrun Valley where we spent several wonderful days walking and climbing in the area. The only time that the Tourist Tax has ever been collected from us was the morning after a night spent outside the railway station at Sedrun.

We reached the top of the Oberalp Pass at 6,642 ft where we spent the night, intending to climb the next day up to the source of the Rhine. Unfortunately we were forced to give up before reaching our objective. We think that we had, as usual, chosen the more difficult and longer route. A strong icy wind suddenly struck us as we came round a bend of the mountain, making it extremely unpleasant and dangerous to continue, so we retraced our steps back to Bondo. The weather was becoming colder and colder, but we decided that it was too late to drive down the steep pass to Andermatt. How much warmer it would have been down in the valley.

We were having our supper when suddenly one military vehicle after another drove up, parking all around us – jeeps, troop carriers, supply transports, etc. We became completely surrounded by the Swiss army on autumn manoeuvres.

During the night it started to snow. How sorry we were that we had not driven down the pass in the evening. We worried that it might become slippery and even impassable. We had to get moving at first light.

What a run around we had next morning to find the soldiers whose vehicles were blocking us. We were finally directed to the officer in charge who gave orders to release us.

*

A Home on a Barge

Taking a walk along the tow-path of a French canal, on the banks of which we had spent the night, we came upon a young man sketching. Always interested in other artists' work I approached him and to my surprise found that he was an Englishman. He pointed to a barge moored at the side of the canal and said that it was where he and his wife lived permanently.

He invited us in and proudly showed us around their comfortable and tastefully designed home which he and his wife had converted from an old run-down barge. His wife was busy at her sewing machine. She makes and dresses puppets professionally and he sells his pictures. We were invited to stay for tea. They proved to be a most charming couple. They remarked how inexpensive it was to live this way and the cost of their 'home' on the water was far less than the cost of any other conventional home – their only expense being the price of the canal sluice-gate tolls when they move from one canal level to another. The network of canals and rivers in France are navigable from coast to coast, i.e. from the Atlantic to the Mediterranean.

*

A Home on a Yacht

Also in France we met Kim, a young Hollander. We were conveniently camped on the harbour of the yacht club at the very fashionable Mediterranean resort, Grande Motte. Moored near us was a long, slim, red ocean-going yacht with a very tall mast, named *Athene Nike*. We were admiring it curiously when a young man came down the gangplank and introduced himself as Kim, the captain of its two-man crew. The boat belonged to a wealthy industrialist and he and his Egyptian crew-mate maintained and sailed the boat.

Kim invited us aboard to their quarters, a rather cramped and not very tidy bachelor establishment, and introduced us to his mate.

Kim came to dinner the next evening. In response to our queries about his job on the yacht he replied that he loves the sea and enjoys his job away from routine work in crowded cities of northern climes.

*

Circus People

Another early morning experience as a result of hunting after dark for somewhere to sleep, as so often happens to us when visiting a city. We are so busy sight-seeing that we forget that we do not have an hotel in the city to go back to and evening suddenly comes upon us, by which time we are rather tired and hungry too. That evening when we returned to Bondo parked in a city square we approached a woman getting into her car and asked which direction to take to the caravan camp. She kindly told us to follow her, and though we passed what we considered to be a suitable spot in a lorry park, we did not want to be rude and ungrateful, so continued to follow her until at some point we lost her in the traffic. So we drove around and suddenly saw two huge caravans parked in a side street. We decided to join them.

I had risen at dawn to wander around when a 'bear' loomed out of the mist. However, we were not sleeping in a dark, wild forest, but next to a cemetery in Oslo. Following the 'bear', a large black furry dog, was a little lady who stopped to talk – fortunately she spoke English, a Hollander married to a Norwegian. I walked a little way with her so that she could show me where the nearest shops were located.

When I came back to Bondo I found Do speaking to our three Austrian neighbours. It turned out that they were a travelling circus group, husband and wife team and their partner, a younger man. The latter excused himself – he had to go and do the shopping. We were intrigued to see him take out of his caravan the tiniest motor-bike on which he drove off. The husband went off to tinker with his car.

The woman accepted our invitation to come in for a cup of coffee. She was charming, with oodles of personality. She and her husband were a comedy act and their partner was a clown.

Sometimes they performed on their own and at other times joined a circus. She said that they had been on the road for many years and had performed in many countries. In fact, quite recently they had been in our part of the world with the Italian circus, Merano. She herself was a third generation circus performer. "It is a hard life", she said, "but we love it." They particularly enjoyed coming to Scandinavia as they loved the people here.

We would like to have heard more of their experiences but the young clown had returned from his shopping expedition and she had to go and make breakfast for her menfolk, and they would be driving off immediately thereafter.

We also had our breakfast before driving off.

*

Another Inveterate Traveller

John (from England), our next-door neighbour, shared the shade of the only large tree on the Lugano car park and later the lakeside at Locarno. He was travelling in a Mini-Morris van accommodating himself and bicycle. He enjoyed Bondo's 'spacious' hospitality.

Resulting from his cycling reconnoitres we chose the Maggia valley for most of our stay in Ticino.

By profession a ventilation engineer he manipulates his working life to satisfy his passion for travel far and wide; competitive marathon running, rowing, mountaineering, skiing and rappelling.

It is a joy to receive his long, interesting letters penned in the most beautiful, meticulous and artistic script.

His latest letter tells of having just built an 'own design' sculler.

*

Fun on a Fjord

After leaving Orsta on our Norwegian visit that year we drove to Seeboe and crossed to the Nordingsfjord and arrived at Oye at the end of the Vardingfjord, where we stopped at the pier where two motor-boats were moored and decided to spend the night there. As the evening wore on more boats arrived, so we moved away from the pier to some open ground nearby.

On awaking next morning, to a perfect day, we saw that dozens of boats had arrived – obviously for a rally, so we thought we should move on. However, Bondo the Britisher, who always attracts, was the object of a charming Norwegian family – husband and wife and three young sons, ages ranging from fifteen to ten years. Ann, who is a Scot, approached us – Knute her husband originates from Oye and they live in Alesund. They met in South Africa where Ann was teaching so, of course, there was an immediate bond.

They invited us to join them on their boat for a cruise on the fjord. Knute told us that the Union Hotel at Oye was the last of the nineteenth-century hotels to which the British aristocracy still come to stay and as a young boy he drove them in a horse-drawn buggy. We spent a most enjoyable day with them on their boat, ending with a supper of fish caught by the boys.

*

Our Quisling Guest

Whilst living comfortably in Frognor Park in Oslo we innocently entertained, before breakfast, a Quisling who walked his dog every morning thereby making our acquaintance. He told us that he had fought against the Russians in their invasion of Finland before World War Two. As he wanted to continue the fight against them he joined the Germans when they invaded Norway.

However, punishment was meted out to him after the war and he was incarcerated for six years by his own countrymen. He kindly gave us an excellent map of Norway and Sweden as a parting gift.

*

Encounter on the Mountain Top

One of our most useful stops on our journeys back and forth to central Switzerland is the parking place at the side of a deserted wooden hut used it seems, occasionally, as a club house for a shooting range.

It lies in a flat, green, open, fertile valley in the Bernese Oberland, below steep forested mountain slopes and protruding above, the sharp pinnacle of the Stockhorn. In the distance a wonderful view of the famous high peaks of the Jungfrau range.

We had always been fascinated by this strange shaped peak which we had first seen in the distance across lake Thun and then found we were parked in its immediate view, from what we have come to call our 'shooting-box camp'. When we observed through our field glasses that a cable car reached the summit we decided to do just that.

We drove down, entering the narrow Simmental Valley between more strangely shaped mountains which led to the village at the bottom of the cable car. We settled Bondo in an attractive position on the car park overlooking the village fields in the valley below the opposite mountains – excellent for a night's stay when we came down on the last cable car.

Two separate cable cars took us to the top. The first was to an upper valley with a small lake, apparently a fisherman's paradise. Everyone, young and old, seemed to be carrying fishing rods. There the majority alighted.

On the second cable car we reached the rocky pinnacle itself. There was the usual restaurant. From a ledge the hang-gliders were jumping off for an ideal flight from this high point.

We climbed higher up natural rock steps through an Alpine Garden (each group of plants named) to the very top. On three sides there was a sheer drop with only an iron bar for protection – what a view! But tantalising when the clouds began gathering – swirling around the peak, disappointingly blotting out the world below.

It was a strange, rather mystic feeling as though we were alone floating, detached in the sky. Everyone else had climbed down. Then a couple emerged climbing up out of the mist. She was most incongruously dressed in a long flimsy divided skirt. We remarked jokingly, between ourselves "How impractical for a mountain climb." We were a little embarrassed when they came up to us "Oh! you speak English!" (we still do not know if they heard what we said).

He had a strange English accent which we could not immediately detect, she was obviously Swiss. When in answer to the usual query "Where do you live in England?" we said we lived in Israel, she asked excitedly, "where in Israel? I was a volunteer in my youth in a kibbutz near your home town, and am still in contact with friends there after all these years."

The bond was complete; we climbed down together to the cable car.

His unusual English accent was soon explained when he told us that he was born and brought up in India where his family had resided for several generations since the time of the British East India Company. Neville himself had later lived in England and in Canada.

He had met Gretty on a ship which he had boarded in the Far East, when she was returning from a visit to a sister in Australia. It had been a shipboard romance. A year later they married and Neville joined Gretty in Switzerland. They live in Gretty's family home just south of Bern.

When we arrived down the mountain we invited them in for a cup of coffee. Gretty disappeared, returning from the village laden with goodies for supper – how typical! We were later to learn Gretty never came to visit without generous gifts of jams and tarts made from the fruits of their garden.

They stayed till almost dark. We parted with a warm invitation to visit them in their home.

And so with an encounter on a mountain top began our newest friendship. When we got home we visited 'Gretty's Kibbutz' where after all these years she is still remembered with affection. How gay she must have been as a young girl in those days, and now at sixty is still full of almost youthful life and warmth for all those with whom she is in contact. Neville, after twenty-five years in Switzerland is still looked upon as an outsider and our meetings represent for him a chance to speak English and to exercise his lovely English sense of humour that perhaps the staid Swiss villagers do not appreciate. We have since visited them in their attractive old wooden home and they have visited us in different places.

They have just visited us again. They drove sixty-five km, at a minute's notice, to our 'shooting-box camp' symbolically below the peak of the Stockhorn.

*

Rendezvous on the Rigi

Having arrived at one of our favourite 'plots' on the car park of the *teleferique* above Weggis we were busy levelling Bondo, on the rather sloped ground, with the newly acquired wooden wedges, when we were approached by a gentleman carrying a box of tools who asked us if he could help. His caravan was parked nearby. We were to learn that this was just another proof of Norman's wonderful kind character.

We invited Norman and his wife Heidi for drinks in Bondo. They stayed until midnight, telling us about themselves. Both had lost spouses and had married only three months previously. They exuded happiness. Heidi is Swiss and Norman is English. Heidi had inherited a simple family *hutte* on the Rigi where she had spent all her childhood holidays. She had married an Englishman, who was tragically killed in a motor accident leaving her with two small sons. Norman had married a widow with five small children in order to help her bring up the children. When his wife was dying after a long illness he lovingly nursed her to the end. The children of both have grown to adulthood, and Norman has now become a tower of strength to Heidi's sons.

Both deserve the happiness they have now found, sharing their interests and their activities. Heidi is a weaver while Norman, with a talent for woodwork among everything else he can do with his hands, makes small looms for Heidi's weaving and they sell their crafts at craft fairs, with much success, all over England.

The following day they invited us to go up to the *hutte* with them and to stay the night. Norman borrowed a two-wheel hand cart from the Rigi Kaltbad post office to carry their goods, which they had brought up from their caravan. We followed a wide path, all helping to push the hand cart. When we reached the path leading down to the *hutte* there was much laughter as we manoeuvred the hand cart down the steep narrow path.

The *hutte* is a crude wooden chalet with one room serving as lounge, dining room and kitchen and a half upper floor leading to two bedrooms by wooden stairs. An ancient cattle trough outside serves as bathroom cum kitchen zinc. Also outside is a chemical loo. The ground falls away and we could just see the lake far below.

Norman started up a fire, with wood he had cut during their last visit, and we dined sumptuously on heated-up Marks & Spencer ready-made food, and chatted well into the night.

It was hard to believe that only forty-eight hours earlier we had not even known of each other's existence, and already a warm friendship had developed.

Several days later Norman and Heidi visited us at our favourite campsite by the lake at Sisikon.

When we came to Britain the next summer we stayed with them in their home near Bury St Edmunds and spent a day together at their summer cottage on the Harwich estuary.

From there we intended going on to Scotland. On inquiries Norman found out that the night bus from London would be passing through Milton Keynes at midnight. He insisted on driving us all that distance at night. What kindness!

The next summer when we visited England they were so tied up with craft fairs that we were unable to meet, but during telephone contacts Norman told us that they had acquired a new caravan with a red body and white roof, which he was busy fitting up for greater comfort.

Early that autumn we had to return rather unexpectedly to Weggis. On reaching the *telepherique* car park for the night – lo and behold! there stood the red caravan with white roof and GB number plates. Very excited, we parked 'next door'.

Next morning we took the cable-car up to Rigi Kaltbad. There was a thick mist on the mountain and we could only see the trees a few yards ahead. It was silent, almost mysterious – there was not a living soul around.

We could not remember how far we had walked with Norman and Heidi, but at last we recognised the large conglomerate rock looming out of the mist. We knew that at this point we had to find the path down to the *hutte*. It was very slippery and we were relieved when the *hutte* became visible through the mist.

How we surprised them when we emerged sliding out of the mist – and what a wonderful reunion. We spent a most enjoyable day together in front of a log fire imbibing the wine we had brought to celebrate this unexpected rendezvous.

That evening we all went down the mountain for a farewell dinner party with Bondo, and Norman and Heidi departed for England next morning at dawn.

*

Tatiana of the Mountains

We arrived at Riddes in the Rhône Valley and took up residence on the car park of the cable-car with the intention of going up to Isèrables, the mountain village that nestles on a high shelf on the slope of the mountain. The sky was slightly overcast, so we decided instead to explore our immediate surroundings. We walked through the outskirts of the small town and through the vineyards and orchards towards the mountain. As we crossed a small bridge over a rushing stream that cascaded its way down to the valley we noticed a young girl accompanied by a large black dog. She had heard us speaking English so came up to us and introduced herself. We walked down the hill together. Her dog did not really welcome us as he had now ceased to be the centre of her attention, rushing ahead and disappearing among the vines to annoy her. Tatiana invited us to come home with her and taste her brother's wines. He now runs the family vineyard. It seems that almost everyone in this town owns the vineyards that surround it. Her home, where she lives with her parents, is a very charming modern house set in a beautiful garden among the vineyards. The wine was delicious.

Tatiana worked part-time at a bank in Sion. She told us that she would be free the day after next and invited us to go up the mountain with her.

The next day we took the cable-car up to Isèrables. We were charmed with this little mountain village with some beautiful wooden chalet-style buildings on either side of cobbled lanes rising with stone steps. We noted that shoppers carried their supplies from the small modern super-market in their traditional large wicker baskets on their backs. In the little museum we saw the wicker cradles and the padded bonnets worn by the women for balancing the cradles on their heads.

As Isèrables is high up on the west-facing slope of the mountain flowers and plants are giant size, having sunshine long after it is dark in the valley.

The next day Tatiana fetched us and drove with tremendous speed and skill up the steep winding mountain road, with views overlooking the wide flat valley with its patchwork of fields, vineyards and orchards and then on up a dirt mountain road. After passing a forest of giant larches she parked her car, and led us along a rough path that climbed up the mountain. We looked down on that well-known resort of Verbier far below and across to the snow peaks in all directions. It was bitterly cold, and at one stage we were enveloped in a fine mist cloud. We crossed over thick matted grass and around rocks– no need for a path, Tatiana knows her mountains – and overlooked a nearby mountain with a tumble of rocks covered with green lichen. "I love my mountains," declared Tatiana with enthusiasm, "and I know how lucky I am to live here."

When we finally returned to the car Tatiana announced that we would go to visit her father. Since his retirement from the postal service he has built a buvette high up in the mountain, which in summer serves mountain walkers and skiers in winter. Tatiana, no doubt, inherited his love of the mountains. The place was charming. Mr Laurenti had built it himself, beautiful stonework without and all the woodwork in the interior, with an ingenious rounded bar-counter so that guests could face one another.

The porch has glass walls and roof – lovely and warm, excellent for the winter. In another building are dormitories with built-in beds and bunks most cleverly designed. We were invited for lunch served on the sun porch by Tatiana and her father – charming hosts.

On our return 'home' Tatiana suggested that we move to the thermal baths below Saillon, down the valley. Here we found lovely parking between fields and vineyards. We also benefited from the use of the baths. Next day we reciprocated her wonderful hospitality for a special lunch with Bondo.

The following summer we returned to the area. We parked on our usual site at Sion, which happened to be just behind the Bank where Tatiana now worked full-time. After work she drove us up through the Old Town to a grassy slope between Sion's two famous rocky peaks four hundred feet above the city, each crowned with its episcopal fortress. Incidentally this is where we took up residence with Bondo on our very first visit to this historical town some years ago. We mention in our chapter 'Cultural Capers' that we had attended an International Organ Festival in the Valère Church on another visit.

We had dinner in the Old Town in a very typical Swiss Restaurant with a very typical Swiss menu, after which Tatiana led us through the alleys of this ancient section of the town, deserted at that time of night. The next day we were invited to lunch by Tatiana's mother, and Tatiana drove us to Riddes – at her speed – where we were received with warmth by her very charming and elegant mother who served her speciality, a maize-based dish.

Yet again a lovely encounter and new friends.

*

Swiss Hospitality

A few days later we were to experience yet another example of traditional Valais hospitality.

We were residing on the car park reserved for motor caravan visitors to the famous St Leonard underground lake, when a lady from one of the adjacent houses of the village came and presented us with a large plate heaped with grapes and most delicious plums from her garden. In appreciation I painted for her a picture of the beautiful view from Bondo's window and from her house. Before we departed – another gift, a large bottle of home-made wine.

Guests before Breakfast

A pit-a-pat of tiny feet on the roof of Bondo every morning during our stay on the Isle of Skye reminded us that breakfast was awaited by the large seagulls that inhabit the area. We had stayed here for several days looking across at the Cuillin range in all weathers and all times of the day and night, witnessing dawns and sunsets of sheer beauty in those there hills "over the sea to Skye". Clouds above the Cuillins at sunset like rays from the sun – blue sky and clouds all shades of grey to almost white – the mountain a clean silhouette of navy blue and green showing up even at twilight.

*

We spend so many nights on the eastern shore of Lake Neuchâtel, and often when we wake in the early morning we are surrounded by hundreds of gulls pecking away in the grass. Suddenly they rise into the air en masse and minutes later return to continue their breakfast.

Then there are the swans – those truly majestic birds – our most frequent and welcome visitors even before breakfast – ready to grab from our hands. They give us endless hours of delight watching them relaxing on the water, poking among the reeds at the edges, wings puffed up like stately galleons, taking off by first running on the water, off on a short flight to land far out on the lake. We have also had the joy of seeing them with cygnets riding on their backs. When the cygnets become tired of following Ma and Pa they climb aboard.

Of other birds, perhaps the most unexpected were some Rhode Island and Orpington hens who visited us on the parking site at Pitlochy where we had spent the night after an evening at the famous theatre there.

At Yvoire, that flower-bedecked French village on Lake Geneva, having parked after dark, we were awakened by the crowing of cocks to find ourselves next to a fowl run – the birds eagerly watching us hoping to share our breakfast.

*

At the tiny village of Shieldaig, a National Trust property on Loch Torridon in the Western Highlands of Scotland, sheep are part of the population. They take up residence in the doorways of unoccupied houses. They are a scruffy lot, apparently belonging to nobody and never sheared. They are fed by the kitchen maid from the only hotel in the village every morning and evening with kitchen scraps. It is quite a sight to watch the sheep and the gulls mob her, the gulls screeching above and the sheep almost pushing her off the rocks into the loch. As the gulls grab most of the scraps because they are so much quicker, the sheep, appetites unsatisfied, make for our caravan to share our breakfast. We dare not open the doors as they do not wait for an invitation to scramble in – we are not prepared to be that hospitable as they are rather smelly, which is rather an understatement.

*

There are the beautiful reddish-brown squirrels, with enormous tails, in the park in Geneva where we are wont to spend our nights when we visit that city. We watch these busy little creatures running across the grass, stopping to give us a curious look, asking what we are doing in their territory so early in the morning, then scrambling up the enormous tree under which we are parked. And not forgetting the grey squirrels in the Park at Bath – another of our night camps, adjoining the Botanical Gardens there.

*

The least welcome morning visitors are the dogs, invariably followed by man or woman swinging a leash. We object to them using our wheels as a latrine (in several places we have seen dog lavatories provided by the municipalities). But mostly the dog owners just allow their pets to perform anywhere while they stand watching them with

the utmost affection and concern if they display any symptoms of
constipation or diarrhoea. We have, of course, made the acquaintance
of some of these dog owners on occasion – sometimes very interesting
and extraordinary people.

*

Oldenvatn Geese

We were determined to visit the Briksdal Glacier which we learnt was
one of the highlights of Norway. In a land so extravagant in natural
phenomena we wondered how anything could be more wonderful than
what we had already seen.

In spite of persistent bad weather we are fortunate in always being
'at home' with time to wait for more favourable conditions. Because
of such delays we have often had experiences that we might have
missed had we adhered strictly to plan.

That afternoon when we drove up from Olden on our way to
Briksdal and parked at the top of the Oldenvatn Lake the weather was
so threatening that there was little point in moving on. We were
obviously on private property. We asked and were granted permission
to stay on this land belonging to the small *bygd* (village) – a few
houses, each a different colour, with typical Indian-red farm buildings
with ramps to the lofts, surrounded by agricultural land and wooden-
fenced paddocks. A tongue of the glacier and the cleft of a dark
mountain was the backdrop to the valley beyond the *bygd*. The soft
sound of distant waterfalls and the river flowing into the lake could be
heard.

The lake was flanked by mountains with the green fields of little
farms near the water's edge and forests up the slopes.

The lake, fed by the river coming off the glacier, varies in colour
through every tone of turquoise with the changing light as the massive
clouds move above it.

When the wind drops the water is so still that the mountains are
reflected down in their entirety. It rained most of the night.

In the morning our first guests came towards us across the water.
Four magnificent Arctic geese with long black necks, black heads with
white sides and brown wings with black tails reflecting into the quiet
waters, causing just the slightest ripple as they swam so delicately

Norwegian Fjord Horse comes to say 'Hullo'.

Uri and Uriella demand breakfast – Sisikon

across a patch of turquoise water, at that moment illuminated by light coming through the break in the clouds. I wondered whether I was dreaming. No, it was morning, I was awake and looking out through our window on this lovely vision. The geese waddled ashore, like swans, so comparatively ungraceful and less romantic when they are ashore, pecking greedily at something in the grass. They seemed to resent the two black crows who were there ahead of them, one stared defiantly at the geese before flying off in disgust. The four geese did exactly the same action at the same time – raised their heads, stretched out their large, beautiful, brown wings; rested from pecking at the grass, all facing the same direction – strange behaviour. They eyed Bondo suspiciously. Above us a flock of tiny birds made a swinging movement in flight.

We wondered whether they were the same geese that visited Rhayader every summer as described by Paul Gallico in *The Snow Goose*.

*

Fjord Horses

The next morning we had very special guests for breakfast. There were four cream-coloured Fjord ponies grazing in the paddock. Unable to contain their curiosity, two of them came over to investigate. One of them put his head through our front window looking at us with his large brown eyes and what seemed a friendly Hullo! We fed them on apple peels and carrots – obviously only a snack. Then one of them stuck his head through the door, started licking the green seat cover and a green cushion and then tried to have a go at our new yellow and brown plastic table cloth. He then withdrew his head and rubbed himself on the side rear-view mirror.

The Fjord Horse is a breed particular to western Norway. Anyone travelling through Nordfjord can hardly fail to notice how proud the locals are of their very own breed of these charming light coloured horses. We had already seen these attractive little horses working in the fields, drawing the hay carts, and in the days following we would see them pulling the two-wheeled traps taking tourists up the winding steep road to the glacier.

We, however, walked up.

*

Donkeys

On the shores of Killary Lough in Connemara early one morning, we had the funniest guests – two scraggy little donkeys with their pelts hanging in patches like untidy torn rags on an old tramp. We thought that they were suffering from a skin disease, never before having encountered donkeys which shed their coats according to the season.

They were so sweet and friendly as they peered so appealingly through our open back window at our laid breakfast table. We shared our breakfast with them which we all enjoyed.

*

Sisikon Ducks

For several years now we have returned to one of our favourite spots on the very edge of Lake Uri, that part of Switzerland associated with the legend of William Tell. The village of Sisikon lies on a little peninsula that juts out into the lake, backed by a steep valley which rises into the mountains.

On our first morning we wake to movement on the grass around Bondo. Our old friends the Mallard ducks are there to welcome us. We share what we can of our bread. They quack with satisfaction and blink their beady eyes at us. When our bread is finished they waddle off to the edge of the bank, about two metres above the water, flap their wings, landing on the water with a splash and swim away. Gulls too are much in evidence flying low above the water and now and again diving to catch a fish.

It does not take long for word to get around. The ducks return accompanied by their friends; the males with deep turquoise coloured shining necks and side feathers and the females spotted brown. One after another they fly up from the water to land on the grass bank quacking expectantly round us.

As soon as we are ready we go off to the village shop, select what we require for ourselves and ask for bread to feed the ducks. With sympathetic understanding the shopkeeper goes to the back of the shop and returns with an enormous bag full of stale rolls. Not only do our guests come for breakfast, but often come also for lunch and dinner – we have counted up to more than twenty at any one time.

Sometimes they come to meet us when we return 'home' from one of our mountain walks and follow us making us feel like the Pied Piper of Hamelin.

Our ducks are an integral part of our lives at Sisikon every year. They are so good for one's sense of humour. They are such funny, absurd birds the way they waddle when they walk and hurriedly peck, peck with their big yellow beaks in the grass. When we feed them they grab a crust too big before anyone else gets at it, shake their heads and wriggle their necks in an uncomfortable attempt to swallow the crust whole. Greedy, silly creatures – but when they spread their wings and swoop, oh so gracefully, on to the lake and swim with so much dignity on the shimmering water, then rise up into the air and fly away together over the lake they are not funny – just beautiful and a part of the glorious scene.

*

Uri of Canton Uri

Uri, the lone swan at Sisikon, occasionally visited by a fellow swan, is our most regular guest not only before breakfast but at all hours – waddling ashore and knocking at Bondo's door demanding his ration of bread rolls. Uri prefers to eat out of my hand so that in the process of greedily grabbing he can nip my fingers. He then shakes his long neck vigorously in the effort of swallowing. When I think that he has had enough or the bread supply runs out Uri has the impudence to express annoyance by either trying to attack me or waddles off in a huff.

When he comes on the water he is too low down the embankment to be fed by hand and he is not as good at catching bread in mid-air as are the gulls which gather around.

We have named the swan Uri, but is it a he or a she? On land Uri displays all the arrogance of the male and also the ungainly pigeon-toed waddle of the overweight female – but, when gliding gracefully on the lake or flying above it with wings outstretched Uri represents nature's perfection.

French without Tears

We had spent so much time on the south-eastern shores of Lake Neuchâtel, and though we had driven through, we had never actually visited the city of Neuchâtel so attractively situated on the lake below the Jura Mountains that separate France from Switzerland.

First we would visit La Chaux-de-Fonds, the town in the mountain above, the birthplace of Le Corbusier, to see the exhibition commemorating one hundred years since his birth in 1887, also to see the famous clock exhibition. Instead of climbing the steep road up we left Bondo at the Neuchâtel station and went by train.

After a very interesting day we returned and drove down towards the lake to find a suitable park for the night. We had noticed on the way in a sign to a sports centre. We came to a small car park at the edge of the lake surrounded by enormous trees. This proved most suitable. The excellent conveniences of the sports centre were no further than on a camp-site. Beyond the car park an open area of rolling lawns and gardens stretched back from the lake to some very attractive public buildings – which we were to discover next day to be the University. We spent a most comfortable night alone on 'our' car park.

The next morning we walked through the park into town. We slipped into the tourist office for information and guides to the town. Among the material we were given was an announcement about the Summer French Language Courses that would take place the following month at the university.

We knew that Neuchâtel University was famous as a language school and that Neuchâtel people boast that they speak purer French than the French. With our perfect accommodation this was a wonderful opportunity. I had attended French courses with very limited success; when I try to speak I am hopelessly tongue-tied and the fast-speaking French are difficult to follow; Lynn managed only a little better with her school French.

We had no specific plans for the next month – so why not? We would think it over – a month's intensive French! What a lovely dream I had that night – suddenly I was speaking fluently to all and sundry. I was assured next morning that you don't speak French in a month.

We were charmed by this lovely city and its old town and climbed up the hill to the very beautiful old château and cathedral overlooking the town and the lake and the beauty of the surrounding countryside beyond.

We returned 'home' via the university (we were two minutes away), changed into our bathing costumes and dived into the lake for a refreshing swim and then sat sunning ourselves on the rocks and fed the swans.

We left Neuchâtel the next day, allowing ourselves a week to consider.

We sent in our applications and returned in time to register. On the forms we gave our Neuchâtel address simply as Motor-Caravan Bondo, Lake-side, Neuchâtel. Perhaps the secretary was puzzled, but as always, the Swiss are discreet and ask no questions.

We were given a written test to determine to which class we would be assigned. It should have been an oral test, then I would have been assigned correctly to the baby class. Lynn was one grade above me. And so began our university life at Neuchâtel.

My classmates were a mixed bag, all under thirty, some under twenty – I did feel rather spare. The youngest were recently graduated high school students from German-speaking cantons all over Switzerland with a good grounding in school French. The foreigners were a Japanese, a South American, a Spaniard, a Korean, an eccentric older American woman and a young English woman whose husband was a South African working in Neuchâtel (whom we later visited).

It did not take me long to find out I had been placed in too high a class.

My teacher encouraged me to stay in her class promising, as she certainly did, to translate into English anything I did not understand, and the office said it would be stupid to change as I had the best teacher on the course. But in competition with my fellow students it was rather disconcerting and confidence-shattering to be the dunce of the class, especially when most of them could have been my grandchildren. I did my homework religiously with Lynn's help.

We enjoyed the excursions organised for the students on the lake and walks in the mountains.

In an article in the local press they wrote about the two "elderly English ladies" who attended the Summer Course and lived in a caravan down by the lake.

The course did not turn out to be the magic formula for French fluency, but we did enjoy our comfortable lakeside 'Hostel', our daily swims and entertaining new friends in Bondo.

*

Getting by with French

When foreigners mispronounce in English we can usually understand, but when we mispronounce in French why do French speakers not understand us? Presumably they do not even understand us when we speak ungrammatically – perhaps snobbery on their part!

Even though we can shop in supermarkets without the need of French, sometimes one cannot find the article one requires in these enormous shops, so one is forced to ask in one's best English accented French. Fortunately, there are often fellow shoppers who hear the English accent and who know some English and do help out.

The funniest experience I encountered was at Portalban, a popular Swiss lakeside resort where a farmer milks his cows by hand behind a sophisticated restaurant in the centre of the village. Veal sausages were available in the deep-freeze self-service, but as I saw some in the butchery section of the supermarket decided on the purchase of fresh sausages, so pointing to the large white sausages, "*Bonjour, Monsieur – ces saucissons – est-il veau?*" The butcher's reply – in English, "I do not understand English" – my reply – "*Mais maintenant je parle francais.*" I again repeated the question – "*Est-ce-que ces saucissons sont veau?*" He again replied that he does not understand English, implying that he understands German and Italian. At this point the owner of the shop came up and said "*veau*" is pronounced "voh" – no different from my pronunciation of the word – the same as "*eau*" for water! How do the French pronounce "though" – as I pronounce "*veau*"? The shop owner informed us that her daughter is in England studying art at the Camberwell Art School. Hence her better knowledge of English, no doubt!

On another occasion in a large Migros supermarket I could not find the margarine – so asked the young assistant – "*S'il vous plait, ou est la margarine,*" which I pronounced with the usual soft 'G'. She did not appear to comprehend, so I repeated the word with varying emphases on the three syllables and with hard and soft 'G's. She remained uncomprehending for some while – finally she said – "*Ah! Margarine*" with a long Maa and hard 'G'.

When we wanted peanut butter – difficult to remember the word "*cacahouettes*" for peanuts, so we tried "*beurre noisette*" – near enough! Without success. Perhaps I should have asked for "*beurre singe*[1] [pron: sangsh] *noisette*"!

After all I did obtain 'B' grades for French and Latin in Matric in 1066!

---

[1]   *Singe* is a monkey.

To France Again

We decided to visit old friends at Firminy. On reaching the river Rhône we crossed over on a long bridge in this very wide section of the river to the village of Andance where we camped on the river bank and watched, fascinated, the large barges making their way upstream attached to one another forming a long train. It is a pity that there is not more river traffic on this very navigable river instead of so much road traffic.

As we sat contemplating this wide stretch of water we thought of our romance with the river Rhône, over the years during our lives with Bondo, from its source at the famous Rhône Glacier in Switzerland to its meeting with the Mediterranean.

The highlight of the day was watching the game of Jute – the tilting match – which we had never before witnessed. Players stand up on long thin boats with long thin poles with the object of pushing their opponents off their boats into the river.

The next day, after a beautiful drive over a fifteen-mile pass, we arrived at the home of our friends, our second visit with Bondo. We were most warmly welcomed and manoeuvred Bondo down the driveway to suitable parking at the side of the house.

We spent several wonderful days with them visiting this rather lovely part of France, the farms and the villages with their small, attractive Romanesque churches, in one of which soft recorded music is played continuously. The inhabitants of the village of Chambon sur Lignon, at great risk to themselves, saved escaping maquis and Jews during World War Two. They took Jewish children into their homes as part of their families, thus saving them from the Nazis and giving them loving care.

A little museum with many photographs and letters illustrates the story of this island of humanity during the ugly years of the Nazi occupation of France.

A memorial plaque in French and Hebrew honours the village and its brave people.

Some of the villagers were invited to plant trees in the Avenue of Righteous Gentiles in the gardens of the Holocaust Museum in Jerusalem. It gives us great pleasure to read the name of the village of Chambon sur Lignon on the plaques beneath those trees.

One of our hostesses was a nun at a convent during World War Two where the chief Rabbi of Paris was hidden by being employed as a gardener at the convent – at the time only the Mother Superior knew his identity.

We enjoyed a festive dinner with the family to celebrate Bastille Day and our farewell.

In the evening we all went to a '*Spectacle Vivant*', depicting the story of the country of the Val Grangent, overlooking the gorges of the Loire, where the performance was held against the background of the restored Castle.

Next morning we set off at 6 a.m. having bade our farewells late the night before; only Benedict was awake to wave us good-bye.

We took the road that would lead us along the Route des Dauphins to Geneva, stopping for a late breakfast and a short sleep.

After passing through La Côte St André, the birthplace of the composer Berlioz – unfortunately the museum was closed on that day – we arrived at Virieu in the late afternoon where we found the Municipal camp – a feature in France of small caravan camps on the outskirts of villages, invariably near some attraction such as interesting châteaux and churches. We have also stayed at the camp near the source of the Seine and found the birth of that famous river – a small spring oozing from under a rock shaded by huge trees.

Here at Virieu we decided to stay the night. In the event we stayed four nights. The reasons were two-fold. First we found this little camp very pleasant; of the ten permanent caravans parked there only four were occupied. Secondly, we had run out of cash in French francs, and on inquiring about a bank were informed that there is no bank in Virieu, only a banking agency which operates for a few hours twice a week. That day they were already closed so we would have to wait another three days.

During those days we also ran out of food, but killed a couple of tins which we keep for such emergencies. Normally we consume only fresh food. We also had the time to wash Bondo's curtains, hot and cold water being available at this camp site day and night; and at last make the linings for the curtains with material bought some years previously in a street market.

And, of course, we discovered and visited the château at Virieu, famous for spanning eight centuries of occupation with numerous interesting architectural and interior features added during those centuries; also famous because King Louis XIII stayed there in 1622 on his way back from signing the Paix de Montpellier. The château is presently occupied and owned by descendants of the original owners.

So when the bank agency opened for business we were there, but they refused to cash Travellers' Cheques, and only after a telephone call, to whom we know not where, they agreed to cash a twenty US dollars banknote, out of which we were able to pay for the camp accommodation, fortunately very inexpensive, and some petrol to get us to the next town.

We departed after very friendly farewells from neighbours with whom there had been lack of meaningful contact owing to the language barrier. But the children bid us "Good morning" and "Goodbye", the extent of their knowledge of English of which they were very proud.

And off we drove in search of a bank!

Another Year

As usual our travels that year were again rather unplanned. We wanted to go to Norway again, but in the event it was too late to go as we feel that one must be there by midsummer's day, the latest.

However, we had a wonderful summer. We arrived in Switzerland the first week of July and after a visit to the Gruyère area and a few friends, we were unable to climb the Moleson due to bad weather.

Then a quick run through France spending a couple of days only in Paris as our wonderful 'camp' behind the Petit Palace was broken up by a whole squad of police – too many campers there at the time – but we managed to pay a visit to the Pompidou Centre for the first time. Architecturally the glass and steel structure looks more like a high-tech factory than a Parisian cultural centre – but inside there is so much of interest. We were specially impressed by the beautiful and restful interior and the many advanced facilities of the library.

The highlight of that visit to Paris was the exhibition of horses at the Grand Palais, the theme being the 'Horses of St Marks', one of which was on loan to the exhibition. There were all sorts of equestrian exhibits; some wonderful sketches of horses by Leonardo da Vinci (1452–1519) on loan from the Queen's collection and the 'Boy on a Horse' from the Athens Archaeological Museum, where we saw it again on our way home in the autumn.

From Paris we went to Normandy. We spent a few days at Caen, comfortably 'accommodated' on the banks of the River L'Orne among glorious old trees and overlooking the race course. Three-quarters of the city had been destroyed during World War II. Whole suburbs of modern buildings, especially in the port area, bear witness to this fact.

Fortunately the great cathedrals, although there was some damage, have been completely restored. Of the several churches that we visited, among them the Abbey of St Etienne with its imposing façade and thirteenth-century spires, attached to the massive Abbaye Aux

Hommes, which was founded in 1066 by William the Conqueror, it is the smaller Church of St Pierre (1490–1510) that stands out particularly – its gracious single tall tower; the fine proportions of its high gothic interior and the delicate and intricate details of its internal ornamentations.

We found most moving the bronze statue of 'Phoenix Rising from the Flames' in front of the reconstructed University building which was completely destroyed during the World War. Caen retains its cultural, intellectual and artistic centre that it has been since the Middle Ages.

It was exciting to visit Bayeux. In recent history it was the first town to be liberated by the allied invasion of 1944 and so, for a while, it had the distinction of being the capital of liberated France. For the British it was the reconquest of 1066. The Tapisserie tells the whole story of William the Conqueror's invasion of Britain on the seventy metres of the eleventh-century masterpiece appliquéd on linen. We had the time to study and enjoy it in detail.

We camped in the shade of 'L'Arbre de la Liberté,' an enormous plane tree planted in 1797 on the Cathedral square. How convenient for us to attend the organ and clarinet concert in the Cathedral that evening – and what a glorious Cathedral, the interior with its high gallery of thirty-five arches surrounding the altar – filled with the sound of seventeenth-century music. An unforgettable evening. This Cathedral is among one of the most beautiful in all France with its three steeples, a Gothic elevation above a Romanesque nave. The original cathedral was consecrated in 1077 in the presence of William the Conqueror and his wife Queen Matilda.

Then on to the D-Day landing beaches at Arromanches and to see the detailed model of Mulberry Harbour overlooking the remains of the actual Harbour. From there we went to Sainte-Mère-Église where the American parachutists landed during the night before D-Day. It was in this village that the film *The Longest Day* was filmed.

At the Airborne Museum, a most impressive structure with its roof the shape of a parachute and inside a model of a parachutist hanging from the ceiling; also interesting exhibits and some memorabilia of parachutists who took part in the invasion. Here we met the curator. He had come back to live in Sainte-Mère-Église, having spent his working life with the American Army, and to marry the woman with whom he had been billeted in the weeks after D-Day – she then had a husband and four-year-old son, but when he visited some years later he found she had become a widow.

He put us into his car and drove us around the area showing us the details of the landings with all the tragedies that went with them. He has written two books, recording the story, copies of which he presented to us. We have maintained contact with him over the years.

After the couple of weeks in Normandy we crossed the channel from Cherbourg to Weymouth and spent a couple of weeks in Devon and Somerset seeing friends and making new ones and also having repairs made to Bondo. We had just limped into Somerset with the clutch about to give in. Leaving Waterloo Cross camp, after friends had visited us there, we visited Killerton House and Bickleigh Mill and Castle from where we returned to Taunton to have Bondo serviced. Rather than going all the way to Scotland we decided to visit North Wales instead. We did a few lovely walks near Golgellau, the Precipice Walk and another in the Elan Valley; and we climbed to the top of Snowdon.

It was very cold on top with no visibility on the west side, and we had climbed up the east side of the mountain. There are several ways up and down – we went up the Miner's Track, where copper was once mined, rather a tough climb over boulders in parts. We came down the Pyg Track over toward the beautiful Llanberis Valley, from where we had superb views back towards the Miner's Track. The Llanberis Valley runs towards Caernarvon where we subsequently went, also to Anglesey and Conway. We also visited the interesting Dinorwig Quarries near Llanberis.

We made an interesting human contact too – a couple from Bath whom we met at the foot of Snowdon. They invited us to visit them, which we did and they gave us two days of their wonderful hospitality, spending one whole day showing us around Bath.

From there we went on to London where we spent almost a fortnight and saw some good theatre. Then back across France where rivers were in full spate as they were also in Wales. We then spent the last weeks of our stay in Switzerland enjoying the glorious autumn colouring.

Orages (Storms)

Storms are not uncommon experiences in 'Life with Bondo' and some have been very frightening.

One night when we were camped high up on the Jaun Pass, in the Gruyère area of Switzerland, a violent storm broke and for well over an hour we were bombarded with hail stones the size of pigeons' eggs. The noise was horrendous, we sat stiff with fear that damage to Bondo's flimsy fibre-glass body would, at any moment, let in a flood of water – fortunately all was well and the ordeal passed with Bondo intact.

In Ullapool, on the Scottish West Coast, a gale-force wind threatened to topple us. Every tent in the nearby camp was blown over and the drenched campers had to be evacuated. Fortunately we were parked in the town, so we were able to move in between two buildings and thus weathered the storm.

After a perfect cloudless day up on the Gemstock above Andermatt, and next day the drive through the narrow gap of the Reuss Valley and the Devil's Bridge below the Gotthard, we were parked at a village railway station at the end of the valley, when later that evening we were struck by such a violent wind storm that one of the windows on Bondo's roof was blown away. We were forced to seek shelter for the night on the station platform behind a shed. At crack of dawn the railway officials arrived – they were not amused – we made a hasty retreat.

A carosserie in the area put a temporary cover on the open roof, as a new window to fit our Bondo could only be obtainable at the other end of Switzerland.

In the Val de Ferret, Valais Alps, we had climbed to the glacier at Fouly during the day and were warned of the coming storm by other walkers we met coming down from the mountain.

During the night we were awakened by loud and continuous rumbles of thunder, now and again a louder boom, the lightning flashing so intensely that it lit up the entire mountain reflecting the brilliant white of the glacier. The sheet-lightning was so continuous that it remained alight with almost no break, only interspersed now and then with the most blinding fork-lightning from one end of the mountain range to the other. This then was the *orage* that the climbers had been warned about – but it came only several hours later. What a terrifying experience to find yourself up in the mountains in such a storm. It was terrifying enough down below to experience this fantastic phenomenon. The electric storm went on and on for we do not know how long. It seemed it would never end. To watch it was quite blinding, but to miss it for one minute would have been a pity.

Suddenly the rain came down in a deluge and the lightning illuminated the sheets of water like a curtain which blotted out the entire scene. As the rain eased off the sound of the river, hidden behind a high bank of avalanche rubble, was a continuous roar. We could clearly hear boulders being rolled along the river bed.

We hoped that there would not be another avalanche like that which devastated this valley in 1981.

A Few of our Feats of Endurance

> Great things are done
> When man and mountain meet
> This is not done
> By jostling in the street.
>
> William Blake

Orphans of the Storm

We spent the next night at the end of the road at the stone marked
GRAND COL DE FERRET intending to attempt the climb to the col the
following day. It was a clear, calm night with a view of a moonlit
glacier.

We set off at 10.30 in the morning, descending a short distance to
the river, crossed over on a wooden bridge and followed the mountain
road up on the opposite bank for about a hundred yards when we
found a *sentier* rising steeply through a veritable alpine garden, a
steep, narrow and very stony path, a shortcut which led us back onto
the road very much higher up. The road had taken sharp hairpin bends
to reach this point. We could see Bondo far down in the valley below.
On the brow of the hill the road led to another sharp bend, but we left
it and took another path leading very steeply upwards through a gap to
a col high above us. The vegetation through which we climbed was
dense. There were flowers taller than ourselves, slippery rocks and
marshy ground under foot. It was very hard going. If we thought this
was The Col we were very much mistaken.

We reached the top after one and a half hours and continued over
rather rough ground on a fairly level area. In the distance, beyond a
shallow valley, on the rise opposite was a long stable. As we
approached we could hear the soft tinkle of cow bells and peeped in.
There were a few cows feeding in their stalls. There was no one
around. In the yard outside there were three long drinking troughs in a

row, water flowing from one to the other, indicating that there were large herds up in the mountains. We did not see any, they could have been anywhere in this vast area.

Beyond the stable we started climbing steeply, picking our way carefully along the many eroded cattle paths that criss-crossed the slope. It was a hard and difficult slog, the paths, such as they were, clinging to the side of the mountain fell away hundreds of feet into a deep valley below; and above us the never ending undulating green of the alpage.

We rested for a while on a comfortable 'couch' of soft moss surrounded by minute flowers and in contrast some tall yellow thistles. We contemplated turning back, but decided to carry on at least to the next rise, hoping to see some sign of our objective – *The Col*, but there was always yet another and another rise with nothing visible beyond. We asked some walkers passing us on their way down how far we still had to go. One group said twenty minutes and another one-and-a-half hours. "Ah, but then you will see Mont Blanc." There was no question, we would struggle on! There were clouds behind us, perhaps it was even raining down there, but ahead it was clear.

Across the deep valley to our left the side of the mountain dropped down in sharp diagonal layers of naked rock, above which were tan-coloured sand slides where snow had only recently melted and above that the black crags of the mountain tops. Behind us the moving mist and clouds allowed us the occasional glimpse of the white peaks of the Valais Alps, but not clear enough to identify the familiar forms of the Grand Combien and beyond the Cervin (Matterhorn) and Monte Rosa.

At last the path began to level out and walking became easier. Ahead of us now we could see the mountain and its glacier peeping above the slope. The whole area of uneven folds of morrain was covered with short grass and tiny flowers, at one point masses of tiny white daisies. We are always amazed that the higher one climbs in the Alps the floral wonders become more and more minute.

Here and there shallow streams covered the path which we had to cross on stepping stones. The vertical sides of the path were broken away exposing diagonal layers of thin black slate, a minute replica of the valley slopes on the opposite side.

On a high ridge in the distance we saw tiny moving specks of people. At last it seemed we were approaching The Col. We climbed down a wet slippery path before finally struggling up a rock-strewn hill to reach the top of The Col. What a sight! High above us on our right were the sharp, dark peaks of the Dolent (12,420 ft) and on its slopes three enormous glaciers, the tongues reaching down below us. The one nearest to us is actually the shape of a huge tongue (now we really understood the term 'tongue of a glacier'). The glaciers are clean and dazzling white. In the valley on the Italian side far below us the silver thread of a river meandered into the distance.

On the top of the Col at its highest point stands a stone beacon marking the border between Switzerland and Italy and its height above sea level 2,537 metres (8,245 ft). It was 3 p.m., four-and-a-half hours since we had left Bondo. We had climbed 2,720 ft. Next to the beacon was a large flat brass disc with arrows pointing in the direction of the peaks giving their names and heights and an inner circle of arrows pointing in the directions of Europe's capitals and distances from this point.

We sat down on the soft grass to rest and partake of our meagre meal of bread and cheese, an apple and a carton of rather insipid cold tea – and to contemplate the glory of the scenes around us. Clouds hovered over the peaks, covering and uncovering them. We were facing the Italian side of the Mont Blanc massif and as the clouds shifted for a brief moment we caught a glimpse of the great white mass that is Mont Blanc. The highest point visible most of the time was Mont Jorash (13,086 ft).

A few climbers with their backpacks came up mostly from the Italian side. This col is part of the classic 'Round Mont Blanc Three-country Route' starting and ending at Chamonix. The path zigzagging up is not as steep and shorter than the direction from which we had come. Believe it or not there were even a couple of mountain cyclists, the latest sport. Most of the time they have to carry their cycles and when they ride they look ridiculous bumping along the rough paths balancing with their feet on the ground.

After lunch we climbed two more hills above The Col. We probably reached 2,600 metres! We had a better view of Mont Blanc, but only for a brief moment. Looking back towards the Swiss side nothing was visible now. Dark menacing clouds were gathering. It was already 5 p.m. – time to make our way back.

When we came down to the stable, which we reached at about 6 p.m. – we had hurried from the col to try to beat the oncoming rain – the sky above us was very dark and menacing. We wondered whether we should seek shelter in the stable which would mean going down after dark. Dogs barked at us, the farmer came out. I asked if he thought heavy rain would fall soon, it was already drizzling. All I understood from his reply was "*La Fouly est plus loin.*" Perhaps he was inviting us in. However, on the spur of the moment we decided to battle on down. Battle was no exaggeration because the descent from the stable was very steep and difficult – so many deep and eroded cattle paths. From the stable to the so-called farm road we had to walk down into the valley and then up the hill a short distance before reaching the road which we intended to follow down. We saw the backpackers on the hill, who had passed us going down before reaching the stable (we and they the last climbers on the col), opening up their tents as it was now raining quite heavily.

As we reached them the storm broke with bursts of thunder and lightning. We looked at the road a few yards beyond and saw a virtual river flowing down. We donned our flimsy packamacs and opened the umbrella in the wind. We were ignored by the six people putting up two pup tents, one larger than the other small one. They had to scurry and take their gear inside. Eventually they all disappeared into the tents while we huddled together under the plastic umbrella; and then it started hailing in addition to the downpour.

We thought that perhaps we should seek shelter in the stable, but we were already too far away and would have had to climb down into the valley and no doubt wade through rushing water before climbing back up to the stable.

In sheer desperation we knocked on the 'door' of the small tent and begged to be let in. At that point, as the occupants opened the outer flap, the wind caught the plastic umbrella, turned it inside-out and the plastic cover came away. We were told to leave it outside and our haversacks and macs in the outer section of the tent. We crawled to the back of the tent; being thoroughly sodden we dripped water onto the floor of the tent. While we began to remove our wet boots and socks the two girls started wiping the floor in an attempt to dry it; we, of course, remained wet and freezing. They offered us biscuits. We felt most embarrassed imposing our wet presence on them.

The heavy rain, thunder and lightning continued on and on. Eventually the girls, who had been polite enough not to change their wet clothes immediately – also because the four of us were so cramped in the tent – probably decided they were feeling too cold and changed their tops for sweaters. At some point during the storm the companions in the next tent came to say they wanted to make coffee – but the girls had the coffee and they had the stove, etc. Result, no coffee!

At about eight o'clock the rain eased off, so we decided that we had outstayed our welcome and must attempt to get going. With their help we crawled out and put on our packamacs. Lynn rescued the broken umbrella, wound the elastic round the metal ribs and carried the plastic cover. Fortunately the river running down the road was now only a trickle. It had obviously come from higher up the mountain where the rain had started earlier.

We decided to run all the way down along the road in order mainly to get warmed up, also necessary as we were wearing our sodden boots. The zigzag road was washed away in parts – this mountain road served the stable. After running for about an hour and warming up in the process we came to a point where the road was completely washed away. We had earlier passed the second sentier up which we had climbed on the way up and found water rushing down it, so then realised we must stick to the road. However, about two hundred yards before reaching the washed away section of the road we had passed our first sentier which we now had no alternative but to go back to, as we could not cross the mound of mud and stone which was once the road. We descended the sentier carefully picking our way over wet, slippery stones on the path and reached the road just above the wooden bridge. Fortunately this had not been washed away because it crossed the river at a fairly level part of the valley.

We reached Bondo at about 10 p.m., exhausted, soaked to the bone and freezing. We lit our heater, ripped off our wet things, put on dry clothes and lit our stove to prepare for ourselves a nice hot soup.

We had noticed a few parked cars and a Hollander family near one which had its engine running. We had presumed they were just about to drive off. The father came to our window and told us that they, too, had been caught in the storm coming down from the Grand St Bernard Col and were soaked through and were running their car heater in a vain attempt to dry themselves before starting their long walk back to the camp. Only then did we find out that the bridge had been washed away and that we were completely cut off. We offered them hot coffee but they preferred to get started as it was already so late and they had a long way to walk to Fouly.

As far as we were concerned we were delighted (*camping sauvage* for one night only was allowed in this area). Now we had a legitimate excuse to stay in this lovely place alone and at home in all our glory. We hoped that we would remain marooned for at least a week. When we examined the damage the next morning we were well satisfied that repairs to the bridge might take even longer. We had not taken into account Swiss efficiency. A new bridge was in place in three days!

The kind farmers at the stable just above us sold us fresh milk, *serac* mountain cheese (pressed cottage cheese) and half of their large loaf of bread.

We undertook two more wonderful walks, one through the valley and another up the mountain towards the Grand St Bernard Pass before driving away across the new bridge.

Val de Ferret

*

Grand Paradis – Roc Coupé

We set out to reconnoitre in the lower valley of Grand Paradis at about 2 p.m. There were sign-posts on the corner pointing to Roc Coupé and Rosetan, but no indication of the times it would take to walk there. So we set out for a stroll entering the forest along a saw-dust strewn path, no doubt a bridle-path, then up a gravel path that started to become steeper. We were following the course of the fast-flowing river and into the forest. We came to the path signs to Roc Coupé again, crossed a small bridge over the river and then the narrow path turned steeply. We could not resist our usual curiosity and climbed on, the path becoming steeper and steeper, tree roots across the path forming natural steps. Our stroll had been forgotten and we were on our way up for how long and for how high we could only guess! We would go up as far as the Roc Coupé and return– so we thought!

We passed other walkers, all of them coming down. The climb was very steep, but there was relief from time to time when it levelled up. The forest was thick on both sides of the valley and very deep down the sound of the river a faint murmur.

We struggled on and up, resting often. The path was rough with loose stones and from time to time very steep. The sheer rock face of the mountain towered above us. We could no longer hear the river, lost in the dark forest now very far below us. Then the path passed precariously over scree that fell away almost perpendicularly down the mountainside above and below us. We walked across it rather gingerly, it was frightening to look down and better not do so– a false step and that's it!

As we came beyond the scree the path led under the great overhang of dark black rock– Le Roc Coupé. We walked on the level under its dark shadow and black, damp trodden floor. It was exciting, the great mass of the mountain above us and the sheer drop down the rock face. We were certainly cut down to size. Beyond the overhang we started to climb steeply again between the enormous trees. The path by contrast was softer underfoot with fine brown pine needles. Another steep pull up and we reached a grassy slope and into the sunlight. We sat down to rest, exhausted by the effort and the excitement of it. We met a young girl on her way down. We thought that, by now, we ought to know where we were heading, as it seemed that the end of the climb need not necessarily be the Roc Coupé. She told us that after another short climb we would reach Rosetan (we thought it might be a restaurant) and then we would be on the level until we reached a waterfall and the rest would be easy going down to Boneveau.

After we had rested and eaten our apple – we had made no provision for spending so many hours away from Bondo– we went to the edge to look down. We were in the very cleft of the mountain we had looked up to from our car park. We could not see Bondo, but could just see the back of the parking area. The climb was not yet at an end, but admittedly not quite so steep. We came out of the forest again into a wide open area of green alpage extending to the edge of the sheer rock wall of mountain face, broken here and there by a narrow rounded shelf of pale green alpage. We searched the slopes looking through our binoculars as surely this was ideal grazing ground for chamois and deer and about the right time of day, now after 5 p.m. We had passed a large wooden farm house, Rosetan, with no sign of life. We wondered where the farmers were. There was also no sign of cattle on this ideal grazing area. We walked on, relieved to be more or less on the level. In the distance we could see the waterfall coming off the glacier and dropping from a great height into the valley below.

We had a wonderful exhilarating feeling, almost spiritual, so far up at about 5,500 feet, the wide open green area well above the tree-line giving a sense of spaciousness. The massive rock walls of the mountains above us and the world so far down below gave us one of those moments of gratitude to be alive and for the experience and the sensation of being away from it all. I find it difficult to find the words to describe it. Perhaps it needs a poem?

The waterfall still appeared to be a long way off. The path led down roughly along the broken edge of the alpage and then rose again before dropping down to the waterfall, still a formidable way off. We met two walkers, Hollanders or Belgians (Belgians, we consequently discovered, meeting one of them in his car in Champéry a few days later). They said that they were returning the same way they had come, but showed us their survey maps and told us that we would have to climb a col after Boneveau and then return via Barmaz. That did not exactly correspond to what the girl had told us. So we decided to go on as far as the waterfall and for safety sake turn back from there. That would be far enough anyway when we looked back across the alpage and thought of the long climb down.

We reached the bridge which crossed the river over the waterfall, so near the edge that we could not see the drop, but the views back up the cascades and the glacier above the high rock walls were magnificent. Here we met a young family man with pregnant wife and two small boys. He explained that the path led down to the cabin at Boneveau, to which he pointed in the distance, and from there downhill all the way to Grand Paradis. Of course we should go that way. So we went along with them. They came from Champéry. He knew his mountains well, having climbed since he was the size of his youngest boy. He was so sweet with the children, pointing out things along the way.

But before we started down towards the farmhouse it was still necessary to climb from the waterfall. There were times when we really felt it was too much, but on we struggled until the path dropped down towards the house; a typical Valaisian wooden chalet with stables below. We could see the cows inside – at least we would be able to have some milk, we thought. There were a few wooden tables and benches on the terrace and we gratefully seated ourselves in a position facing the glacier which appeared very near from this point. The young family occupied the other table, they were obviously friends of the chalet owner and her daughter. A group of climbers, fully equipped with climbing gear – ropes, pegs, etc. were just finishing their drinks and packing up to depart. They all kissed the young girl and gaily made their way off down the mountain. We did not get our milk, the woman told us she only had enough for her pregnant friend. We had to be satisfied with shandies. Also, she was not serving food, though we intended doing what we had done at Barmaz where we were served a wonderful meal.

We continued on our way, while the family stayed on with their friends. We bade them all farewell, thanking him for his excellent advice.

The rest had done us good and we were all set for the long climb down. It was already past seven o'clock. The path was more or less level along the alpage, passing another chalet where a man was fixing his fences and his large St Bernard dog showed no interest in us. The walking was pleasant and the evening colouring beautiful, exaggerating the green of the alpage and illuminating the glacier; but soon we entered the forest and the path started to descend steeply – the trees were giants, one taller and thicker than the next. The path continued steeply down without relief. At one point the young girl from Boneveau passed with her friend running down the path. Being skiers it was natural for them to speed down the slopes of the mountain. We struggled down leaning heavily on our sticks.

We crossed over a rough mountain road a couple of times, but the path continued down through the forest. Later we crossed a road, the one we had come up part of the way marked *SOUS LES DENTS*, when we had climbed to Barmaz a couple of days previously. We then realised that we were descending the back of the mountain we had faced when we started the climb up to Roc Coupé. We eventually reached the Barmaz road which we now crossed and entered the path towards the other river, crossed the little bridge and arrived home to Bondo, tired but greatly satisfied with ourselves and the glorious experience of one of our most wonderful climbs. It was almost nine o'clock. We had been away about seven hours – so much for our intended stroll!

*

Val De Giffre (Haute Savoie, France)

Having driven up a long, steep haul to reach the Rouget Falls, a spectacular sight, we spent a fairly comfortable night below the falls, in spite of a bad list and loud roar of the waters, cold air and spray and slight wind caused by displacement of air.

Having come so far we decided that we should stay and walk in the area as it was much cooler than down in the valley. We drove on up, and around the first bend we found a clearing just off the road and here we took up residence. After breakfast we set out. We had no idea where we were heading, but finding a path we followed it across a field and into a forest. After about twenty minutes we arrived at an open parking area, the end of the road. Here there were sign boards indicating two walks, one to De Salle and one to Anterne. On a large rock was painted *2 hrs. 30 mins.* We wondered if the timing was the last record run! As usual we calculated on double the time for ourselves.

The path became very steep almost immediately and so it remained for most of the climb. We reached two waterfalls, each emanating from a different source, one falling straight down, the other fanned out over a large round rock – then joining in a single cascade that thundered down the valley – a lovely sight. The rest of the climb was to follow cascades all the way. We battled on, it was tough. Lynn's stiff leg must have been cured at the Yverdon mineral baths, as she climbed as adroitly as usual – taking our time and stopping to take in the beauty on all sides. It was very hot and always a relief when the path went through forest, especially as it was becoming even steeper. After a good hour or more we reached the division of the paths. While we hesitated to consider which path to take we met a family and asked their advice. The woman was very knowledgeable and suggested that we follow the path to De Salle as it was more beautiful and not quite as difficult as the other. We plodded on and wondered what could possibly be more difficult. Lynn had made me a hat out of newspaper, without which I could not have withstood the heat on the back of my head, as the sun was scorching. As we got higher above the tree-line we were more exposed, but fortunately the air became a little cooler. The sound of rushing water cascading down the mountain side had accompanied us all the way. Suddenly we came upon a wide open valley with enormous boulders on either side of the river now flowing more gently over stones into a series of quiet pools.

It was a lovely sight to come across a group of eight-year-olds, or there about – water babies – bathing and paddling in the ice-cold water or sunbathing on the smooth round rocks, and some sitting on a small wooden bridge swinging their legs above the stream.

There were masses of tall beautiful flowers as far as the eye could see, and we decided this was as far as we would go and stopped to have our picnic lunch in the shadow of a large rock. After lunch we decided to walk along the river as far as a wooden bridge we could see in the distance, beyond which we could see the path climbing up the bare mountain-side. "Not for us," we said. We reached the bridge, crossed over and slogged on!

In the distance we could see an overhanging rock and decided to make for its shade and the waterfalls that we had seen from the valley below. We sat in the shade to rest. The Welsh couple, whom we had met in Sixt a couple of days before, were on their way down. They said it was beautiful a short distance further up to the three cascades, but beyond them not very interesting. They had gone as far as the 'Refuge', but Mont Blanc was not visible.

Passing under the rock overhang there was a sheer drop protected by an iron railing. We carried on where the path cut deep into the green edge of the alpage towards the edge of the col where the main fall dropped below us; in its spray – a rainbow. High up on the sheer face of the mountain above us a spout of water shot from under, or through, a rock – beautiful phenomena.

So at last we turned back, satisfied. The walk back, descending steeply all the way was not easy, but the beauty around reviewed and the now cooler air was very pleasant. We arrived 'home' after 6 p.m. We had been away for eight hours. Bondo was very hot, but cooler after opening up to let in the cool evening air as we were, at last, in the shadow of the mountain. We had supper and an early night.

It had been a wonderful day and although a long and difficult climb we were quite pleased with ourselves – after all we have not climbed the Alps all our lives.

*

Robiei (Ticino)

There are certain days which always stand out as special events. Today has been one of them. Such days are usually associated with mountains, and this was no exception.

We had originally intended going to San Carlo by postal bus, but after our trial run to Foglio last Sunday we decided that the road was neither too narrow nor too steep for Bondo. However, today on second thoughts we thought we would take the bus. But while we were still having breakfast the bus passed, so the decision was made for us. In the end we not only drove up to San Carlo, but all the way up to the cable car station. The drive proved quite steep, and it was 2.30 p.m. before we arrived there. Although the day was perfect we realised that it would be stupid to go up the mountain for the afternoon, we needed a full day up there. So we parked ourselves comfortably in a corner beside the electricity pylons. Though there were dozens of cars there during the day, the evening and night are all ours.

We slept fitfully, looking up at the sky and the surrounding mountains worrying about the weather for our walk to the Basadino Glacier at Robiei. We were also castigating ourselves for coming up without sufficient bread to last us the next couple of days as the day after tomorrow would be August the 1st, Swiss National Day, when all the shops would be closed. We decided to ask the postal-bus driver, when he comes up in the morning, to buy some for us to bring on his next trip up. That problem also was solved up on the mountain. We left on the 9 a.m. cable car for Robiei – a very large cabin that apart from a seat fore and aft had standing room for a hundred and twenty-five people. The ballast cabin is for goods with a payload of twenty-four tons – can even take vehicles. Robiei is fifteen minutes by cable car from San Carlo, rising from one thousand to two thousand metres. It was constructed in 1963 and enabled the hydroelectric stations to be built in the surrounding region with its series of high dams. The Robiei Dam is at 1,941 metres.

The cable car rises gradually along the valley and we saw below the rushing river fed by side streams cascading down the steep mountain sides. As we rose higher paths, trees, boulders and a bridge crossing the river became miniature.

We reached the Robiei station at 9.15 and after inspecting the topographical map with the dotted lines representing paths we set off in the direction we chose towards the glacier. The path started up a steep incline zigzagging to lessen the gradient. It was a difficult slog and we felt it would be a difficult descent. There was one other couple and a boy on the path who passed us at some point. Though we attempted to greet them they ignored us as though we were a couple of rocks to be by-passed. Unusual! We went on upwards, the climb more interesting as the path became less rough, passing over grassland and rocks and now and again little streams.

Clouds were covering and uncovering the mountain tops on all sides and we had the feeling that eventually they would close over us. In fact at one point we thought we should go back, as to be caught in the rain or even mist may be unpleasant. We sat watching the clouds covering and uncovering the peaks behind, in front and at the side of us. It was awe-inspiring, even a little frightening. We were alone, no other climbers in sight anywhere. Suddenly three people appeared – two young people and an older man. The older man waved and I remarked in my best German that it looked rather cloudy. He replied that mountains always have clouds and that it is always clearer in the afternoon.

"Climbers", he said, "must be optimistic and always go *up*." We were encouraged to do just that, and how fortunate. We followed on the path somewhat below them. It was lovely now. In the short, almost moss-like grass there were tiny Alpine flowers – the inevitable purple gentian, massed small pink flowers, daisies and the short woody wild azaleas. The rocks glistened in what looked like gold and silver. The snow-white crystal rocks shone like diamonds and were transparent at the thin edges. Outcrops of grey rocks and immense boulders were also part of our environs. To our left we were seemingly closer to the glacier. New peaks revealing themselves and then again disappearing as the clouds played between them. To our right were the enormous serrated naked rock-faced mountains. Far down we now saw the turquoise-blue of the Lake Robiei with its cream-coloured dam wall. High above the lake a bank of white clouds was rising above the mountains, their rocky peaks sharp against the white collars of snow around them and in all the crevices.

Our walk now became even more exciting. Our fellow climbers had veered off to our right climbing upwards toward the rock-strewn wall of a stark mountain.

We were anxious to keep going towards the glacier and were encouraged by noting the white and red markings on a rock indicating the path. We crossed and re-crossed streams rushing from all directions. The air was filled with the soft sound of gurgling streamlets and the call of a single bird. The clouds curled in and out of the peaks casting their shadows across the smooth white face of the glacier glistening in the strong sunlight. We reached the solid snowdrifts under which water had tunnelled its way, and the edges were melting, forming a small canopy against the warm rock as they melted.

The sun was now hot, but one was cooled by the soft breeze coming off the snows. We scrambled over large rocks, jumped the rushing streams and crossed the ice floes. Climbing higher and higher the valley and the dam below were well out of sight. We sat down on a large rock to partake of our lunch. We were facing the glacier! There were large ice-covered rocks breaking through the intense whiteness of the snow. We noticed a rather lovely phenomenon – at the edges of some of these rocks something glistening almost gold in the sunlight, either the melting of the snow causing wetness at the edge of the rock or else crystalline rocks catching the sun, like the small pieces of crystalline rocks which we had collected en route. The shadows of the moving clouds were casting their ever-changing forms across the pure white of the glacier. A saddle of pure white between the peaks had a soft loveliness that one felt one wanted to stroke. We watched fascinated as the peaks appeared and disappeared, the cloud forms and their shadows creating a new picture every moment.

After lunch, in spite of promising ourselves we had come far enough, we decided to try to reach the next ledge for what we might see beyond. But as ever there was yet another and another ledge beyond. At last we reached a ridge from which we were able to look down into the valley below. We then decided there would not be much more to see even from the next ridge so began to make our way slowly back.

The sky had cleared as the man predicted. Mountain ranges out of sight during the morning were now clear, especially the very rugged peaks with their vertical rock faces.

We lost the path markings, but at this point it did not matter. It would be necessary to find it before the final steep descent. Going over new ground, in any case, was more interesting. Finally we struck the path and soon after encountered the three climbers whom we had met on the way up. They showed us some precious stones that they had been collecting – this area is famed for its crystals. The older man told us that he had climbed Table Mountain in Capetown. In fact Lynn always uses Table Mountain's three thousand feet as her yardstick to compare heights of mountains we encounter, as well as how high we actually climb ourselves.

The path down, though steep, was not as bad as we expected. We reached the hotel near the dam about 4 p.m. and went in to buy the bread that the postal-bus driver had told us we could obtain there. It was a large, flat round wholemeal bread of the area. At the same time we were interested to examine the interior of this interesting octagonal eight-storey building. The hotel was simple but cleverly designed with a spiral staircase round the lift shaft and all the rooms radiating so that each had a view. The interior was rather austere – probably just a mountain lodge. We then visited the dam wall, about seventy-two metres high, before taking the cable car down on the fifteen-minute ride home to Bondo. We spent the night again at the cable station.

Next day we went down to the village of San Carlo where we spent the day to await the fireworks in the evening celebrating Swiss National Day on the first of August.

Up in the Mountains

We have described in some detail some of our walks and climbs in the mountains, hoping to share with our readers those inspiring experiences and boast of our feats of endurance and our special adventures.

We must admit that walking in the mountains has become to a great extent the very raison d'être of our life with Bondo and is becoming more so as the years go by, necessitating escape from this noisy busy world and the ever more crowded roads. Life with Bondo offers us the possibilities to live in the valleys among the mountains, conveniently accessible to all the facilities to reach the heights.

In the Bernese Oberland, returning time and again, we have walked in so many different parts, viewing from all angles the great white massif of the Jungfrau and its famous companions, the Monch and the Eiger. We have walked down from the Eiger glacier with the Jungfrau towering above and also from the top of the Schilthorn, walking down facing the great mountain across the cleft of the deep valley. We have climbed up the side of the glacier of the Wetterhorn. From the Schynige Platte looking across to all the peaks, circumventing its gigantic rock outcrops and looking down from a perpendicular cliff to the lakes far below. Up the Stechelberg valley facing towards the Breithorn and its waterfall; the Trummelbach Falls, inside the mountain.

From the Riederalp, to which one ascends from the Valley of the Conches (Goms), one overlooks the Aletsch Glacier which stretches from the Jungfrau for forty-five kilometres to its tongue in the Rhône valley above Brig. It is the largest glacier in the Alps, in Europe second only to the Jostedalensbreen in Norway which we have visited at Briksdal and Faerland, the translucent blue ice similar yet different from the Rhône glacier. The Aletsch Glacier is like a mighty river of ice that fills the entire valley; dark lines swirl in the direction of its 'flow' like the tyre marks of a giant vehicle. In the deep crevices at the glacier's edge the translucent blue of the ice is visible – there is also a tiny dark blue lake. The mountains opposite rise steeply above the great glacier with small glaciers in scooped-out hollows in the dark rocks; there is the distant sound of rushing water as the melting glaciers plunge down in a series of waterfalls which disappear into deep ravines. It is difficult to describe in words the enormity of its proportions and the grandeur of this remarkable phenomenon.

The side of the valley where we walked is a veritable garden of Eden – carpets of massed short-stemmed Alpine flowers, giant trees with bent and twisted trunks weighed down by the weight of winter snows, growing at random among the rocks which they split with their powerful roots and woody azalea bushes in flower, massed against the slope. This whole area is a Nature Reserve, with its forest the highest in Europe. As one walked round the bend the Bernese Alps to the north, now out of sight, and looking south to the distant horizon– the Valais Alps. We could identify the dramatic peak of the Matterhorn (Le Cervin) standing out alone among those other giants of the Valais, Monte Rosa and the Dom.

We know them all at closer range as we have 'lived' in many of the lateral valleys of the Valais south of the Rhône valley as high up as we can drive with Bondo, tackling some steep climbs up many hairpin bends. Many of the Valais villages in the mountains have kept much of their character, the houses built in the traditional style, heavy logs interlaced at the corners, wooden overhanging balconies with movable balustrades to hold the extra hay and outside stairways to the upper floors. Firewood is stored so neatly below the houses that they look like patterned walls. The roofs are of large sheets of rough slate. There are flowers in the window boxes and on the balconies. The village main streets are often so narrow and winding that the postal buses can only just pass through announcing their arrival with the traditional bugle call. Women can often be seen in their national costumes with the attractive little bonnets perched on the top of their heads. It is a pity when some of these villages are marred by tourist development.

We rely on postal buses, mountain trains, *teleferiques* and chair-lifts to bring us high up in the mountains for our walks among the four thousand-metre plus giants of the Valais.

The Matterhorn (Le Cervin)

In these mountains are some of the famous high dams – man's exploitation of nature, amazing feats of engineering – where the waters of the glaciers are trapped behind enormous walls and whose quiet waters reflect the white mountains around them. It is possible, in summer of course, to walk along the paths around the dams crossing the ice-flows and little bridges over streams of melting ice which flow into the dams. In some places water gushes through enormous pipes which are tunnelled into the glaciers. In the Grande Dixence Dam wall it is possible to enter passages to see the giant generators.

Man's ingenuity in exploiting nature is nothing new in the Valais. The ancient bisses are irrigation channels constructed by mountain herdsmen to tap the waters from their sources high up in the mountains before they drop into the deep gorges and channel them to irrigate their *mayens* (high pastures). There are 1,200 miles of these water channels, some still operative, though many of the open wooden troughs have been replaced by less romantic metal or plastic pipes. Following the paths along the bisses is easy and pleasant walking.

Among our most exciting walks and climbs were those dominated by the mighty Matterhorn (4,477 m) not the highest of the Valais giants, but certainly the most dramatic as it stands alone in all its glory, completely detached from the mountains around, perhaps one of the most magnificent peaks in the world. From the Schwartzesee one is overpowered by the enormity as it thrusts its almost pointed mass into the sky above us, mysterious and challenging. No wonder the great climbers could not resist. The stories of their triumphs and tragedies are poignantly illustrated in the Museum at Zermatt.

From the top of the Gornergrat at over ten thousand feet we climbed among the naked rocks and looked across to the Monte Rosa with its Pont Dufour five thousand feet above us, the highest peak in the Swiss Alps. It, as well as several other uncovered peaks, rise out of the mass of ice and snow, with the Gornergrat glacier sweeping down. On our way down, the Matterhorn protruding high above its surrounding glaciers reflected the pink of the setting sun.

The Kleine Matterhorn is like a black point peeping out above a world of ice and snow. The cable-car penetrates it to the station which is tunnelled into the rock from where a lift ascends to the exit. It is said to be the highest cable-car in the world. We were not equipped for walking on the ice – it was enough to circumvent the peak and look down on all sides to the world below.

Glacier de Taconnaz, Mt. Blanc

Fouly Glacier, Val de Ferret, Valais Alps

Perhaps the most dramatic views of the Matterhorn are from our walks from the top of the Sunnega where the mountain is seen from the depth of the valley below to its summit. From here we walked towards Taschalp along an extremely narrow path on the steep face of the mountain dropping hundreds of feet below us– one false step! We battled down a steep slope to Bondo awaiting us at Tasch.

From Saas Grund, in the adjoining valley, we climbed a steep path leading from shrine to shrine, each representing a Station of the Cross, to the church below Saas Fee. Saas Fee lies below those other Valais giants – The Dom, Taschorn and Alpubel.

We have already written about the southern slopes of the Alps in Ticino, our sojourn in the Val de Maggia and our climb to the Basadino Glacier.

Early on in our travels we came to know the Engadine and the snow-covered mountains of the Bernina on the eastern Swiss border with Italy. We have walked in the Austrian Tyrol, lived in the valley of the River Inn and crossed the border from there to the Italian Dolomites.

What lovely walks we have had in the Sedrun Valley and up on the Oberalp towards the source of the Rhine and down to the valley of Andermatt.

In Central Switzerland, now almost our second home with Bondo, we have wandered among the mountains that surround that lovely lake of the Four Forest Cantons (Lake Lucerne) with its shoreline broken by mountain peninsulas and views through its narrow straits to the half-hidden inlets that sweep upward to the high mountains. The famous Rigi is described as an 'island mountain' rising out of three lakes – Lake Lucerne, Lake Zug and Lake Lauerz. Victor Hugo wrote of the views from the top of the Rigi, "that incredible horizon, that chaos of absurd exaggerations and frightening diminutions."

We have climbed and walked in the Vaudois Alps down from the Diablerets and in the deep gorges below the Mauveron and also in the Gruyère.

In France, in the Savoie Alps, we have lived on the river bank in our favourite Val de Giffre and walked among those gigantic cliffs of the Fer de Cheval towering above with their innumerable waterfalls tumbling over the edge – (note our Poem 'Birth of a River').

From the Chamonix valley we have climbed in the shadow of Mont Blanc. We crossed the Vallée Blanche 'the roof of Europe' from

Aiguille de Midi (12,509 ft) in a little gondola (four-seater cable car) to Helbronner on the Italian border with Mont Blanc towering another three thousand feet above us – Europe's highest mountain.

And so high up in the mountains – as one walks along the paths among the flowers on the glistening *névé*, the meadows that lead up to the higher slopes; through the mists and up towards the glaciers we become part of the sublime loneliness and the deep silences. One is at peace with oneself and grateful to be alive and blessed with the sensitivity to appreciate the magnificence that surrounds us.

We bless Bondo who has made all this possible.

Lauterbrunnen Valley – the perfect example of a glacial valley. Below the Junfrau.

Ticino

We spent several weeks in the Maggia Valley. This valley stretches back from Locarno on Lake Maggiore into the Alps with branch valleys reaching deeper and higher into the mountains.

The Maggia River dominates the valley and is fed by tributaries which cascade down the side valleys joining the Maggia in a wide, flat, fertile plain. The river runs wide and shallow during the summer and before dropping down to the lower land around the lake cuts through deep, narrow, white rock cascading over enormous white polished boulders.

There are numerous villages in the Maggia Valley and smaller ones up towards the mountains, picturesque with their blue-grey stone houses with matching overlapping roofs of flat stone, external stone stairways, stone walls and grape vines hanging like curtains over stone-pillared pergolas. Each village has its stone church with spire or bell-tower. The interiors of the churches are richly decorated, the Italian influence is obvious.

The rivers are criss-crossed with picturesque arched stone bridges and precariously hanging footbridges.

The Val de Bavona is said to have the most excellent examples of peasant architecture in the Alps. The village of Fontana in this valley is situated among enormous boulders. There is a stone house which is part of an overhanging boulder which forms its back wall and part of the roof.

The mountainsides are forested with chestnut and other deciduous trees. We went up the different valleys climbing beyond the villages to the alpages above the tree line where cattle and large herds of goats graze all summer, cared for by cowherds who live in rough stone buildings and store the hay in small stone structures which are scattered over the alpages.

The village of Moghegno has the tallest church steeple in the valley. We 'lived' near the village, under enormous trees, at the very edge of the Maggia River.

High up above one of the valleys we had come upon a group of gigantic grey-barked beech trees and from the highest point which we reached some time later we looked down on Lake Maggiore far down in the distance.

Above Bignasco we had climbed above the waterfall which drops down over a sheer cliff to the valley below.

We drove up to Fusio with the postal bus, a picturesque village high in the mountains, the steep road winding upwards in a series of hair-raising and terrifying hairpin bends. We walked on beyond the village through a valley of streams among innumerable specimens of alpine flowers.

For several days we lived outside the village of Bignasco in an open area adjoining the swimming pool – very convenient for our bathes. The village lies at the confluence of the two steep valleys of Bavona and Fusio. The church tower is silhouetted against the forested mountains. The village was within walking distance across the river reached over an arched stone bridge. Above us was the perpendicular rock face of the mountain down which tumbled the beautiful waterfall. In the valley were fields where women from the village worked, drying and stacking hay with long wooden-pronged forks. We enjoyed helping them.

We joined the villagers waiting for Migros' mobile shop which is expected at specified times at each village. You collect a basket, mount the steps and enter the large pantechnicon from the back, go along the centre selecting your purchases from the shelves on either side until you reach the cash desk manned by a young woman; then pack up your purchases, handing the empty basket to the driver as you exit by the front door.

Whilst in this area we also stayed at Verscio to attend the outstanding performance by the famous circus clown Dimitri in his own theatre; also at Locarno for the annual international film festival.

We lived for many days under enormous trees at the very edge of the Maggia river near the village of Moghegno. Here the river runs shallow over white stones with deeper pools in between – most convenient for our baths and even our hair wash. The village of Moghegno has the tallest church steeple in the valley; you can identify it looking down on the valley from high up in the mountains.

Here we met the French-speaking Swiss couple who were camping in the woods nearby, and with whom we have remained friends all these years.

Another feature of Ticino, as a catholic canton, is the many shrines dotted throughout the countryside, some being artistic gems; or Stations of the Cross, each Station in stone, wood or metal reliefs of excellent craftsmanship.

On one of our walks up a mountain side we were amused to come upon the painting of a Crucifixion, at least fifteen feet high, of Christ and the two thieves, with a background of the Mosque of Omar in Jerusalem which, of course, was built by the Moslems about six centuries after Christ. That Mosque is one of Islam's holiest shrines.

We so much enjoyed the weeks spent in Switzerland's Italian canton.

"These Ticino villages of Italian-speaking Switzerland are said to have the most excellent examples of peasant architecture in the Alps"

Cultural Capers

During the years of our wanderings with Bondo we have had the privilege to become familiar with some of the most magnificent and famous of Europe's artistic masterpieces and discover lesser known (and certainly unknown to us) artistic gems that we have come upon quite by chance.

What excitement when we find ourselves gazing upon a famous masterpiece which we recognise from reproductions or have read about or even studied.

Although our final destination is usually known in advance our choice of route is not necessarily so and not even the most direct, as time is not of the essence. Our route may be chosen for pragmatic reasons – to avoid a crowded highway; Bondo's inevitable breakdowns as written about elsewhere; to find a suitable place to spend the night or a deliberate diversion, even a change of course to a point of interest which we had suddenly discovered is not too far out of our way.

Our interest in art and architecture is based, in some modest degree, on our knowledge of the history of art and architecture as chosen and compulsory subjects of our student years. It was the dream of those years to be able to travel to Europe and enjoy those masterpieces in the original. Never in our wildest dreams could we have imagined that we would be able to 'take up residence' in the very shadow of famous cathedrals, in the grounds of magnificent châteaux or stately homes and castles and to stay for as many days as the fancy takes – time to use our small reference library of several art books, including Fletcher's *Comparative Architecture* and books added en route. That we can sit 'at home' with these on the table looking through our window at the object of our study and admiration. The opportunity to come and go, to absorb in detail the building as a whole viewed from all angles at all times of day and night and to examine the intricate sculptural details of their fine portals.

We have the time to appreciate the grandeur of the interiors, the sculptures, the wood carvings, paintings, mosaics, tapestries and furnishings. It is important to see stained-glass windows in varying angles of sunlight, as it is often that only at a particular angle of the sun can a window be seen at its glorious best and illuminating the interior with its very special light.

What luck when we find ourselves in the right place at the right time for a special concert, ballet performance, festival or exhibition.

For example, quite by chance, we had seen a notice that a choral concert would be held that same evening in the Basilica di San Vitale, so we drove the forty kilometres in some haste, reaching Ravenna only just in time to 'take up residence' in the parking lot behind the church, have a quick snack, dress and enter the Basilica. We were overwhelmed by the interior of this ancient, octagonal building with the eight massive columns with their capitals of marble tracery and the famous mosaics, all brilliantly lit. The organ and the choir were high up in the gallery and the voices drifted upwards into the magnificent dome and down to us – the purest and most beautiful sound, as if coming from heaven.

We spent several days in Ravenna whose monuments represent the art of all periods. It was once the capital city of the Goths and then second only to Constantinople in the Byzantine world.

Especially memorable were Dante's tomb in the form of a small temple; the mosaics in the Baptistery adjoining the San Vitale Basilica and those in the church of St Apollinare on the site of the Temple of Apollo.

From there we drove on to Byron's "evergreen woods... at the sweet hour of twilight – in the solitude of the pine forest and the silent shore which bounds Ravenna's immemorial wood... how I have loved the twilight hour..." We woke at dawn, the red sky reflected on the river through the pine trees. Later we went to pay homage at the memorial in the woods built for Dante and Byron.

*

Another chance opportunity was the Organ Festival in the Basilica of the Château de Valère on the hill above Sion with well-known organists playing on the fourteenth-century organ, the oldest organ in the world still in use. Other memories are of the wonderful concert in the Basilica of Bayeux and the ballet performance on Lake La Garda of which we have written elsewhere.

*

It was certainly by mere chance that we found ourselves parked for the night with Constable's view of Salisbury Cathedral through the dawn mist. Our dominant memory of Wells was the Cathedral illumined by a full moon. We also resided on the square of Zaragoza's gigantic cathedral with its many towers and domes floodlit at night. At Rheims we slept in the gardens of the cathedral square and awoke to Jean d'Arc galloping towards us brandishing her sword. At Bourges we were lucky to be guided by students to study in detail the wonderful stained-glass windows which are so famous in this Cathedral.

*

We did not plan to reach the Loire Valley at full moon. We spent one night opposite that pearl of the 'Garden of France', the small Renaissance château of Azay le Rideau, its walls rising directly out of one of the meanders of the river Indre; and another night – Château Ussé with its turrets, towers and terraces bathed in the silvery light of the full moon and reflected in the river below – the perfect image of the fairy castle of the Sleeping Beauty.

.

Still Learning to Live with Bondo

As the years go by we are still learning new ways to improve our comfort in living in our tiny mobile cottage for months on end– only small things. For instance, only this year we discovered the idea of a shoe box as a book-case. Previously every time Do opened her cupboard the books fell out. Plastic containers, in which we buy fruit at Migros, have become so useful for holding our toilet articles, etc.

The heavy bread knife kept in the crockery cupboard above the stove used to fall out dangerously, missing by inches head, arms or hands every time we opened that cupboard. Why not keep it and the bread board, which never fitted well in the crockery cupboard anyway, with the bread in the food cupboard?

For years we lived with our rubbish bin behind the seat, the back of which, incidentally, when lifted becomes the kitchen table. So, when in England we bought another plastic wall bin, (two were previously installed for keeping books and papers) which we glued to the side of the oven – but it kept falling off its glued-on holder! We now secure it with a string.

During the first years we spread our laundry inside the front cabin – finally we decided to use hooked elastic cords, usually used for fastening suitcases to their wheels, by expanding them across the cupboard to use it as a laundry-drying cupboard.

To reduce the rattling of pots and pans while driving we finally packed those not in regular use in a box at the back of the pot and pan cupboard.

Very recently indeed have we discovered that we have a deep freeze – where? – on the top shelf of the drying cupboard with its louvre window, the shelf where we keep our toy revolvers for our protection!

We also picked up a carpet beater in St Anton, Austria, which a housewife had apparently abandoned. Stored on top of the bonnet of

Bondo it proved a source of great amusement to the hundreds of people passing through the car park in Lugano, where we subsequently spent a fortnight. More effective for cleaning our carpets than beating them against tree-trunks or rocks.

Our collection of stones is now kept in flat boxes under the front seat, instead of loose all over the place. And while on the subject of stones, what beautiful colours there are in them – mainly black and white in the Fer à Cheval area. In Ticino the rocks, stones and sand in the river beds glisten with gold and silver mica. The bed of the River Inn had stones of many hues and colours – red, green, yellow, white, black and purple. These stones, which I collect, are a never-ending source of fascination when we live on the banks of rivers and climb in the mountains.

Even our method of bathing has improved. We used to bath in our large basin, first our tops and then our bottoms and legs; now we have added a proper shower by filling a small basin and pouring it over our bodies after soaping all over. The splash on the floor becomes the floor-washing water. Incidentally, hot water is provided from our kettle. We also now have two bathrooms!

Apart from water storage under the floor in three four-gallon containers, which we usually fill at village fountains, we keep four small plastic containers handy to fill with water from various sources. These proved very useful to empty in a hurry when Bondo's engine caught fire!

Iced water, without a frigidaire? Well, last thing at night is to boil a kettle, place it on Bondo's bonnet for the night and at first light empty the kettle of nice iced water into our large Thermos flask.

We had parked for the night outside the Old Forge at Enniskerry, one of the prettiest villages in Ireland situated in a wooded hollow among the hills below the Sugar Loaf Mountain, not far from Glendalough. Horses are still shod at the Old Forge, which is also on the milkman's beat. So we decided to leave our empty milk bottle and cash on the bonnet of Bondo. Lo and behold! In the morning we found a full bottle of fresh Irish milk. Of course, it is only in the British Isles that the milkman still delivers to the door of every household. A lovely tradition!

Because life in Bondo is so comfortable, instead of having had enough of the gypsy life by now we enjoy it and appreciate it more and more each year.

After all Bondo is, in actual fact, a compact five-roomed little cottage with lounge, dining-room/study, two bedrooms, two bathrooms, separate WC, and, of course, kitchen – but not all at the same time!

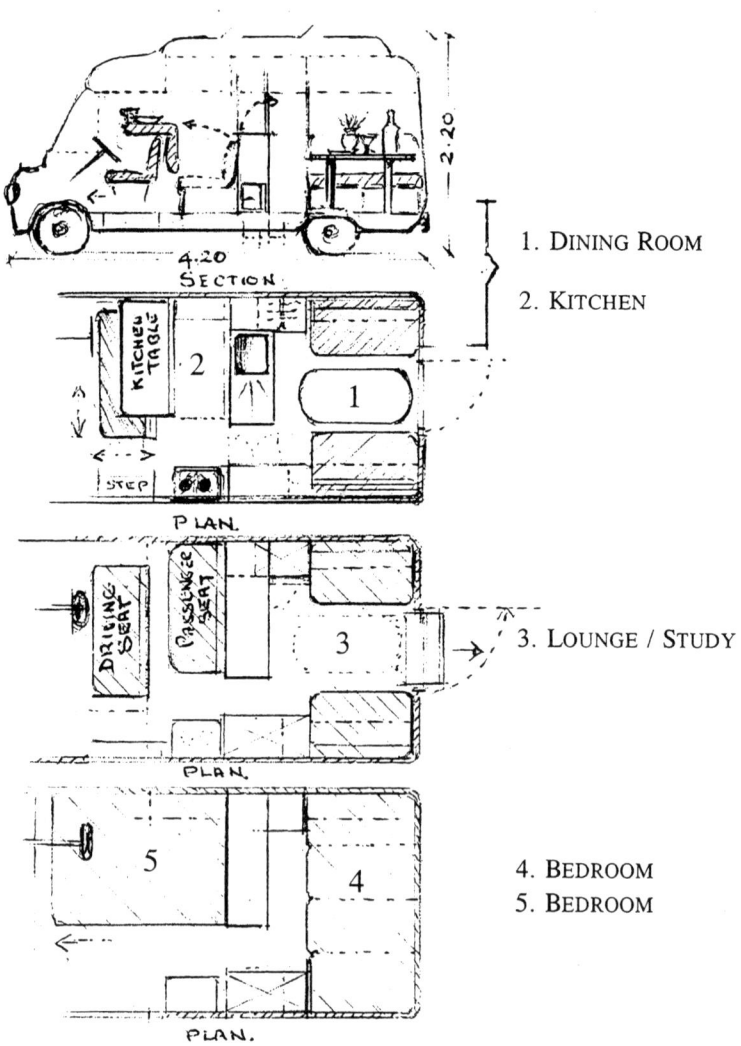

1. DINING ROOM

2. KITCHEN

3. LOUNGE / STUDY

4. BEDROOM
5. BEDROOM

On the Waterfronts

We have often read of and meet people who give up the humdrum of life in crowded cities and buy or build an ocean-going yacht to spend their lives sailing and living on the waterfronts.

Our life with Bondo, or rather part of it, in some ways is similar in that we sail with her (albeit on ferryboats) across seas, fjords, lakes, lochs, rivers and canals and spend time on their waterfronts. What is dissimilar is that Bondo also moves on the land.

Over a period of several years we have lived on waterfronts as far south as Ras Mahamoud at the tip of the Sinai peninsula, from which one explores the wonders of the coral reef – in tropical lands where there is no twilight and the sun drops into the sea like a ball of fire and it is suddenly dark, the sky velvet black with myriad stars twinkling in the crystal clear desert air; the movement of the breeze like a warm caress of comfort after the burning heat of day. In contrast, in the far North we have experienced the day all night with the golden glow of the midnight sun and the long, weird shadows, to the last blaze of pink and gold with streaks of purple tinted clouds and a sea alight when the sunset fades into the soft orange of dawn. With a shiver we curl up under our blankets to have, at least, a little sleep before another day.

We have beached off the Isthmus of Corinth and looked across a navy-blue sea to the grey rocky hills of Delphi beyond. We have stepped out on the velvet sands of the Adriatic coast.

Across the lagoon from the Lido di Venezia is the loveliest of all views of Venice, its domes and towers in a soft golden haze silhouetted against a sunset sky, colours represented so well by the masters of Venetian painting. When the lights go on the reflections are broken into dancing lights as the waters are ruffled by the water traffic passing back and forth across the lagoon. Into the small hours the water taxis (motor launches) bring back the gamblers from the Casino down the small canal and then out across the lagoon heading for

Venice, whether richer or poorer we shall never know. Not long after we are awakened by the chug-chugging of the first barges loaded with supplies, swishing softly on their way to the markets on the Grand Canal. Then the skyline of Venice is illumined by the rising sun.

We have enjoyed the Mediterranean on the south coast of France; and Biarritz on the Atlantic where the rooms with a view at the Hotel du Palais are among the most expensive in all Europe – but we had the same view down the rocky cliffs to the Atlantic breakers on the beach below, with the extra view inland to the hydrangea parks– free, gratis and for nothing.

Then on into Spain – glorious days on the Concha Bay below Monte Igueldo, one of the three hills of San Sebastian, that scalloped shell-shaped curve of beach and surf with its islands which, at low tide, are within easy swimming distance. A step down onto the beach and a swim, the most perfect ever, before breakfast and before the crowds pepper the beaches. Along the Basque coast on the Bay of Biscay where, on the green rounded hills, are the white and red-tiled farmsteads with a backdrop of blue forested mountains. The cliffs drop dramatically and the great waves break among the rocks far down below. Along this coast are busy fishing harbours with their towns of three-storied buildings, narrow streets, thirteenth- and fourteenth-century churches stepped up the hillsides. It is fun to join the hustle and bustle on the quaysides when the colourful trawlers arrive with their Atlantic catch, and when the fleet leaves again for the open sea. Later one sees them far out in groups of two or three throwing the nets between them. At night their lights rise and fall on the great rolling swells – a hard life, no doubt, in the wild seas of the Bay of Biscay, but during the summer the air is balmy and the breakers flop gently on the many sandy beaches.

At Dieppe and Folkestone the same white cliffs are on both sides of the Channel. The loveliest coasts of England are the black rock cliffs of Cornwall, but nothing to compare with the Highlands & Islands of Scotland. That wild, indented coastline with its sea lochs and its land lochs in lovely glens with views to the Islands and the Islands with their views to the Highlands, with skies reflecting ever-changing lights and colours and shadows. The most dramatic scene of all is the late night midsummer sun setting behind the purple-black serrated Cuillins of Skye, silhouetted against a blaze of pink and purest gold cut by streaks of grey-blue cloud and the sea of Loch

Coruisk a brilliant flame. We have experienced dark billowy clouds bearing down upon us – wild sounds of the roaring sea and rocked frighteningly on our springs in the powerful gale, torrents of water lashing against the thin fibre-glass body and roof of Bondo.

The summers in Norway are pure delight – fjords with sheer walls of rock and waterfalls tumbling from the heights above, reflecting deep into the turquoise milky glacial waters of the upper reaches of the fjords. We look up at the glaciers against a clear blue sky, a blinding glare in the midday sun and transparent pink in the midnight sun. These glacier-capped mountains are reflected upside-down with the white reflections dancing as the breeze or a passing ferry ruffles the waters.

Even in Europe's capitals we have lived on the waterfront. In Stockholm, on the Baltic, we spent a week on the shore of one of its islands of the archipelago, not far from the city centre, with a view across the water to the colourful Old Town, the Royal Palace and the copper towers of its famous old churches. Opposite, too, was the berth of the blue and red luxury liners which depart and return from their over-night cruise to Helsinki.

In Copenhagen we stayed on the seafront adjoining the park beside the Gefion Fountain, not far from the little mermaid on her rock, symbol of 'Wonderful, Wonderful Copenhagen'; and at Roskilde, once Denmark's Royal Capital, on the edge of the Roskilde fjord, a deep indentation into Zeeland, one of the three islands that make up that country.

In Edinburgh, beside the Firth of Forth, on one occasion, during the longest day of the year, the late night sun illuminated the wet sands of the Firth at low tide and the water beyond; on another, the bright pink sunset could be seen through the beautiful Forth Bridge at high tide.

In Paris, in the Bois du Boulogne beside the Seine; in Amsterdam on a busy canal in that 'City on the Water' and in Bern on the banks of the river that meanders through that lovely city. In Geneva we faced Mont Blanc across the Lac Leman.

We have lived on the banks of the Po and watched the water traffic on the Rhine and the Rhône, those sealinks from the heart of Europe. On the Loire we have camped where famous châteaux are reflected in the slow-moving sluggish water of that great, much written-about French river.

Lake Uri at the southern end of Lake Lucerne

The village of Sisikon on its peninsular into the lake with the Rigi in the background

Our days and nights spent on lake-sides, too numerous to mention, with diversities of backdrop and weather – sailing yachts reflected in calm waters or fishing boats riding the choppy waters in the wind, mountains appearing and disappearing through rolling cloud and mist – and swans, lovely princesses of the lakes gliding gracefully on the water with imperceptible movement of legs below the surface, their long curved necks bearing small, haughty heads. What a sight when suddenly they spread their great white wings, rise out of the lake, flying low and then touching down again, skimming the surface of the water like seaplanes.

In the bird sanctuary on the shores of Lake Neuchâtel we lie awake at night listening to the nightingales as they sing "of summer in full-throated ease"; by day we watch the waterfowl among the tall reeds at the water's edge.

Gulls are our constant companions – following us across the seas, the lakes, the fjords, the lochs – white wings flapping, flying, circling, sweeping, hovering, perching, accompanied by their shrill cries. While camped on the shore they become our regular visitors, bravely coming closer to share our meals; or in the early hours unsuspectingly waking us with their gentle scratch, scratch sound of their tiny claws on the roof of Bondo. Sometimes at dawn we wake to see them perched by their hundreds on the railings of a pier, then suddenly they all take off across the lake and seconds later they land and ride on the sun-kissed water.

On Lake Uri, at the southern end of the Lake of Four Cantons is our dream camp at Sisikon, to which as long as Bondo is ours we will always return. Here the great Alpine Massif thrusts itself upward out of the deep lake. Vertical rock faces, dark forested ravines with saddles of pale green high pastures, and above the tree-line the harsh world of rough tumbling rock in contrast to the smooth glistening face of the glaciers.

Parked at the very edge of the water we watch the changing drama of the mountains and the clouds reflected in the deep waters. Now there is bright sunlight and sharp shadows; now moving clouds dodging among the mountain peaks or soft mists covering and uncovering them and changing them in form and colour. Sometimes they are reflected in mirrored detail on the calm surface or distorted by the changing directions of the breeze or wind or by a boat parting the waters in its path. We watch the ever-changing colours of the water from pale blue to green to turquoise to royal blue, then almost to navy. Sometimes the lake is stormy with waves breaking against the rocks on the shore at our feet – a perpetual motion of changing colour and light, with every mood of the weather, with every angle of the sun from dawn to dusk and by moonlight. We are in the midst of it and part of it.

These are some of the glimpses of paradise which life with Bondo accords us.

Coming Home to Bondo

Over the many years since we first brought Bondo to Europe, by ferryboat to Greece, we have returned to her every summer by many devious means and routes. Tarrying in one country or another; Greece and the Greek Isles; Yugoslavia (as it once was); Italy, to Venice, Florence etc., and often to visit old friends in Tuscany; via Britain, and once via Finland to the Arctic circle and back across the Baltic sea, always convinced that no travel ever compares with travels with Bondo. No catching of planes and trains and buses, the long delays and waiting for hours for connections and dragging our heavy baggage, finding accommodation and hunting and choosing restaurants – and oh, the expense!

How happy we are to be back 'home' in Bondo – there she is awaiting us at the garage, where she had been brought from her village shed, serviced and checked – and prepared for the road. Off we drive, just in time to collect our mail – and what a surprise! To be welcomed by our dear friend, on relief duty at 'our' village post office, and after-hours, at the back of the post office, an invitation to coffee and to catch up with the news of mutual friends.

Then to the village shop for our first perishable supplies – another warm welcome and a welcome-back gift of a packet of lovely Swiss biscuits. Then for our fresh milk at the village farm depot and to the village fountain to fill up with water. We drive down the hill beyond the village to a favourite parking spot on a farm-track in the forest that leads on to the maize fields beyond.

We are 'home'. We reconnect the gas to make hot coffee with our fresh milk, and a snack for supper (coffee and sugar and other groceries we find, as ever, in our 'kitchen' cupboards).

A perfunctory wash – then out with the bedding, removing the moth-balls from the blankets and the bed-linen from their plastic bags – just where we had left them eight months ago.

We are very tired after our long journey and collapse into our familiar beds exhausted, content and relaxed.

It is so peaceful, just the soft last twitter of a bird. Perhaps the nightingale would sing later – now there is only the gentle rustle of the breeze among the trees and the murmuring waters of the stream below us, and the moonlight filtering through a tracery of leaves.

We awake in the morning to the busy songs of the birds around us. We lie relaxed in bed – no need to hurry – time is now our own, no need even to plan – just to move on when and where the mood and circumstances dictate.

Poems

Our Haven – our Heaven

Of all our favourite sites
'Tis Sisikon that we love best,
Sited on the water's edge
With mountains all around in sight.
Here each year for several weeks
We live in Bondo – home on wheels.
The wheels *they* do not move at all
While *our* legs move on mountain climbs,
Approached on boats across the lake
To where we start those daily climbs,
Wherever varied weather takes us.
But oh! how we love Sisikon,
We're welcomed by the patron
At that campsite on the lake
Where we sojourn every year.

To Ginette

Lake waters lapping
On your beach below your chalet
Where we have found that paradise,
Where ducks abound among the lakeside reeds
And birds among the forest trees.
When it's calm or when it's rough
We go swimming in the lake.
We watch the sunsets
Shining bright across the water,
Spreading colours o'er the sky,
When the sun has dropped behind the Jura
The colours in the clouds above
Just take one's breath away.
At night the rain may patter down,
Or stars shine bright, high in the sky.
At dawn birdsong rings in one's ears,
Day breaks again on Paradise.
The more for Bondo's faults we fear,
The more we treasure her,
To bring us back to paradise
In June of every year,
Where we are welcomed by our friends
Who share with us, their friends and Paradise.

Helicopters in the Lauterbrunnen

There's a cow swinging up in the air,
Why ever is she up there?
I'm sure it is hurting her pride
To be leaving her mountainside
When the weather is still so fair.
How really unkind and unfair
To make such a swinging descent,
Thus missing her part in that festive event
With garlanded horns and swinging her bell,
With friends and herdsmen she loves so well,
Many days walking down, so proud of that feat,
She will miss the parade through her village street.

No longer is timber rolled down to the sites
But swung from above on noisy flights,
Shattering the silence of mountain heights.
Also tourists are swung through the air
For a glimpse of the mountains up there.

Are we losing the mystique of mountain tops
And selling our souls to the helicopts?

Free Eire

We could not afford the delight
Of an Irish farmhouse tea
As the price was Sterling three,
So we had to make do with Bondo tea
Laced with Robertson's ginger jam
From across the Irish sea.
Besides there were many other delights
That we could have for free.
The weather is free,
The clouds are free
With glorious sky effects,
And heather as far as the eye can see
And emerald green when the sun shines through,
And smiling blue Irish eyes
When there are no blue skies.
Hedgerows of fuchsias are free,
And at every turn of the road
Rocky bays and fine white sands,
Purple cloud clad mountains
Across the peat and boggy plains,
And walks on the rocks and sands
With the wind of Eire in our faces.

The Fastnet Tragedy (1979)

After the violent gales,
And the cost of many lives
Of yachtsmen in the Irish Sea,
And several days of heavy rain
The sun came out
And shed its light
To give that famous colour
To the Emerald Isle.

White Cows of the Loire Valley: (the year of the drought, 1976)

"Someone is peeing in our meadow,"
The white cow said to her calf.
"Why do they come to our land now
When everything's withered and stark?
Do they come from a land of plenty
Where the raindrops cool the air,
Where the fields are green and healthy
And the cattle have never a care?
They can hasten now in their house on wheels
To Alpine slopes lush and green.
Do come back to our vale of the Loire
When the 'Garden of France' is more fair."

Sancergues, A Village In The Cher

We shall long remember Sancergues
With its canal and lovely poplar trees,
Where we rested several days
To recover from the drought and heat
On our sojourn to the châteaux of the Loire.
With its poplars rising skywards
And its willows weeping downwards,
White cows, fawn cows, brown and even speckled cows,
But best of all the white cows, a herd of pedigrees,
Seen grazing through the morning mist
And later resting mid the trees.
The spire of the village church
Standing through the centuries,
Soldiers bringing hay
In this year of drought,
The worst in many years.
And the encounter with the family
That introduced us to the Val de Giffre.

Sonnet – White Cows Of The Cher

"Somebody's parked in our paddock,"
Said the white cow to her calf.
"It seems they've moved to our river.
Their home on wheels,
It's white and green,
Perhaps has brought some hay.
Perhaps they're only staying a day
And moving on to greener fields,
If any such there are,
As we have not seen any clouds
A 'rolling o'er the sky.
In any case *we* could not move,
We love our paddocks and our trees
And the river running by."

Birth of a River

Pray let me not take all this for granted.
Living below your towering mountains,
The forests climbing vertically upwards,
The brilliant sun casting deep green shadows
Behind the illumined gold and emerald of green leaves.
The massive grey cliffs of the Fer à Cheval,
Stepping upwards to their serrated peaks,
Their snows and glaciers in the clefts,
The cliffs softened by green sloping alpage shelves.
A dozen tumbling cascades pour down from the melting snows
Glistening white links to the shining glaciers in heaven's blue
Cutting through deep fissures, splashing and dividing
Over rounded rock outcrops,
Dropping into fast-running rivulets far down below,
Rushing and tumbling together in a joyous dance.
We are witnessing the birth of a river:
The Giffre in its new-born freedom
Splashing between boulders, careering over scattered stones,
Widening, narrowing, dividing and joining,
Fed on all sides by new cascades rushing to join her,
Strengthening and gaining momentum,
On its impatient way to join the mighty Rhône.

From The Banks Of The River

But we remain on the bank of the river Giffre
To watch the 'Horn of the Chamois' silhouetted against a sunset sky.
Mount Buet opposite casts a shadow that creeps up
The Fer à Cheval as the sun sinks down.
At night the moon spotlights snow and water against black shadows of
    cliff and forest,
Beneath the dome of heaven spattered with a billion stars.
At dawn, as the last star fades, the sharp outline
Of dark mountain masses, mysterious against a pale translucent sky,
And the small near beauty of sunlight through transparent leaves,
Of soft, lazy twittering of birds hiding deep in the dark, cool forest,
Of brilliant small wonders of alpine flowers and ferns
On the field and forest foot-paths.
The perpetual sound of rushing waters lulling the senses
To all but the magnificence around.
Let me not take all this for granted.

At Home

At home beneath the waterfall
The mountains above us towering tall.
Beside the cascade falling fast
Across the dark rocks, rushing past,
A rolling, dancing, gurgling song
In our ears all day and all night long.

Haystacks

Haystacks shaped like cones
Standing all in rows,
Just like soldiers on parade
Waiting in the sun to dry
Before being carted off
For packing tight inside the loft.
Hay like laundry hanging
On fences long and tall.
Hay baled round and fat
And then stacked end on end.

Lake at Nantua

Three men in a boat
On the lake afloat,
Their fishing rods bent
O'er the water calm,
    Reflected down.
The village beyond
With its little homes,
The mountains above
And the forest around,
    Reflected down.

Having Run out of Gas

Left right, left right
Carrying our gas
Hung on a stick
From the depot
In Lugano
From Via Frasca
To Cassarata.

Left right, left right
Along the road,
Keeping in step
To balance the weight,
Stopping to rest,
Having a laugh.
Our road was long
But 'home' at last.

Memories Of Stockholm

From Venice in the South we came
To that Venice of the North
Built on eighteen islands.
The City Hall, Venetian style,
With its red-brick campanile
Mirrored on the water.

We saw the Viking Wasa ship
On the eighteen bridges tour.
Watched the changing of the guard
In the Royal Palace yard.

From lovely Skeppsholm Island
Over the water the sunrise
Illumines Old Gamla Town,
Its spires and copper-domed churches
And buildings in various hues
So bright in the clear northern light.

Each night we watched the ship glide out
Across the Baltic sea,
Each dawn another ship sailed in
Returning from Helsinki.

By night the lights of the city
Dance on the rippling sea,
Reflected like jewels in the moonlight
From multi-coloured to white.

Last Words

We will not blame you if, after reading this little book, you conclude that you prefer the 'Tourist Trail' with no worries, everything organised while travelling, and every comfort in the hotels and restaurants – in other words, the easy way.

Bondo and ourselves, however, still come up for more again and again – the hard way... and in the process grow younger every year.